The Book of Proverbs in Plain English

In the simplest to understand format with a daily calendar
guide, to help you practice and apply
your daily readings.

Frank LaRosa

authorHOUSE®

AuthorHouse™
1663 Liberty Drive
Bloomington, IN 47403
www.authorhouse.com
Phone: 1-800-839-8640

First published by AuthorHouse 11/22/2011

ISBN: 978-1-4567-9635-8 (hc)
ISBN: 978-1-4567-9636-5 (sc)
ISBN: 978-1-4567-9637-2 (e)

Library of Congress Control Number: 2011915927

Printed in the United States of America

Cover Designer: Damon Bowie
Email: damon@kernstudios.com

Preface

I came to realize that most people avoid reading the Bible because it was just too frustrating and difficult to understand what the passages were saying. I, myself, was one of those people. I would reread the passages over & over trying to understand what the actual message was. When I would discuss it with others, whether in a Bible study, with friends or family, or just in conversation, opinions always differed, making it more confusing to me. The only time I could make sense of any of it was on Sundays, when I listened to the sermons from our church's pastor. But, for me, once a week was not enough, I wanted to understand it daily. How could I learn to live accordingly if I couldn't comprehend what I was reading each day? I bought different Bibles, looking for the easiest to understand, and although some are written in more modern language, I still could not totally grasp what the message was saying.

Knowing there must be many people out there, just like me, looking for an easier understanding, I decided to write this "Book of Proverbs in Plain English". Although the passages were written about 3,000 years ago, the principals and lessons to be learned are still applicable in today's life. As written in the Proverbs, *"Gaining wisdom is the single most important thing you can ever achieve"*.

The Proverbs cover a wide variety of topics that will help you live better and wiser. But, if you can't understand the message, how can you apply them to your life?

This book is written in the easiest to understand wording & format. I took three different Bibles versions, read each passage over & over and reworded them into "plain English", without altering the meaning of the passages. I also added explanations (from research and references) to many of the verses that will help you get the full understanding.

There is no other 'Book of Proverbs' written as simple & easy to understand as this. If you follow the daily calendar chart and find the passages easy to understand, you will look forward to reading these 'words of wisdom' each & every day.

Apply them and see a tremendous difference in your life!

Frank LaRosa

Introduction

prov-erb: *a profound saying, maxim, or oracular utterance requiring interpretation.*

This is the dictionary's biblical meaning of the word. A simpler meaning is: *a short, concise sentence that expresses moral truth.* It comes from the Hebrew word that means, "to rule or govern" and were written to provide profound advice for governing our lives. A basic philosophical definition of wisdom is to make the best use of knowledge. The opposite of wisdom is folly.

The main theme of Proverbs is the nature of true wisdom. Embedded into each human being is the desire to gain knowledge and understanding. Solomon writes, "Fear of the Lord is the beginning of knowledge. Only fools despise wisdom and discipline" (1:7). To have knowledge is good, but there is a huge difference between knowledge (having the facts) and wisdom (applying those facts to life). We can possess all the knowledge in the world, but without wisdom our knowledge is useless. We need to learn how to live out what we know.

Proverbs covers nearly all topics, which include: youth and discipline, self-control, resisting temptation, family life, business matters, marriage, wealth and poverty, immorality, words from the tongue, seeking the truth and knowing God. Proverbs are usually short, mostly in the forms of poems, brief parables, pointed questions and couplets that contain a combination of common sense and timely warnings. Any person who follows its advice will walk closely with God.

All Bible teaching churches preach the Word of God and usually concentrate mostly on the Gospels, which are the actual words and teachings of Jesus Christ. The Gospels give us the truths of how God himself expects us to live and act. But I believe that if more people became aware of the Proverbs and the wisdom to be learned from them, and apply them consistently in their own lives, they would discover how their lives can be more fulfilled and manageable by learning the way to obtaining true wisdom from God.

By reading, understanding and applying the teaching of the Proverbs, it will give you a better understanding of the teachings of Jesus, which were written and recorded nearly one thousand years later.

This book is written in simple, plain text with an easy to follow format. No jumping back and forth or telling you to find reference on another page or from another book, and with "plain English" explanations, you will be able to get a full understanding of the message that is being delivered.

Easiest way to read these Proverbs on a daily basis.
There are thirty-one chapters in Proverbs and most months have thirty or thirty-one days, with the exception of February. I find that the easiest way to gain wisdom on a daily basis is to read one chapter each day, according to which day of the month it is. For instance, if you start on the 1st of the month, read chapter one, on the 2nd, read chapter two and so on. In the months that have thirty days, read the last two chapters on the last day and the last four chapters in February. (see calendar chart)

If you commit yourself to reading daily it will stay fresh in your mind and give you the understanding that the only key to wisdom is knowing God. Not only read the thoughts and lessons, but act on them in your life today!

"The wise person seeks to know and love God"
EXPLANATIONS & IMPORTANCE

1. There are two kinds of people who portray two different paths of life. The stubborn person who hates or ignores God is a fool, while the person who seeks to know and love God is wise.

> *So it is important that we choose God's way and he will grant us wisdom. The Bible is written to lead us to living right, making right decisions and having good relationships.*

2. In relationships, Proverbs gives us the advice we need for developing our own personal relationships with family, friends, and co-workers. In all relationships we must show love, dedication and high moral standards.

> *We should treat others according to the wisdom that God gives us, or our relationships will suffer. To relate to people we need consistency and discipline to use the wisdom that God gives us.*

3. Our speech is, without a doubt, a test of how wise we've become. What we say shows our true attitude toward others. What comes out our mouths will reveal what we're truly like.

> *Self control is needed to be wise in our speech. We should choose our words well and always be honest.*

4. In our work, God controls the final outcome of all that we do. We are kept accountable to perform our work with discipline & diligence, and not be lazy.

> *In using our skills we must never get relaxed or self-satisfied, because God himself evaluates how we live and we should always work with purpose.*

5. Many people work hard to gain money and fame, but, as viewed by God, true success is having a good reputation, moral character and spiritual devotion to obey him.

> *Everything comes from God, including our talents, our resources and our time and we should always use them wisely. Everything is perishable, but a successful relationship with God lasts an eternity*

Follow this calendar guide for reading the chapter relevant to the day of the month

1	2	3	4	5	6	7
Chapter One	Chapter Two	Chapter Three	Chapter Four	Chapter Five	Chapter Six	Chapter Seven
8	**9**	**10**	**11**	**12**	**13**	**14**
Chapter Eight	Chapter Nine	Chapter Ten	Chapter Eleven	Chapter Twelve	Chapter Thirteen	Chapter Fourteen
15	**16**	**17**	**18**	**19**	**20**	**21**
Chapter Fifteen	Chapter Sixteen	Chapter Seventeen	Chapter Eighteen	Chapter Nineteen	Chapter Twenty	Chapter Twenty-one
22	**23**	**24**	**25**	**26**	**27**	**28**
Chapter Twenty-two	Chapter Twenty-three	Chapter Twenty-four	Chapter Twenty-five	Chapter Twenty-six	Chapter Twenty-seven	Chapter Twenty-eight (in the month of February read the last 4 chapters on this day)
29	**30**	**31**				
Chapter Twenty-nine (in leap year, read the last 3 chapters on this day)	Chapter Thirty (in months with 30 days read chapters 30 & 31)	Chapter Thirty-one				

Chapter 1
THE BEGINNING OF KNOWLEDGE

*Solomon is known as the wisest man that ever lived. His
Book of Proverbs gives practical suggestions for effective,
everyday living that still apply to today's living.*

1:1 The Proverbs of Solomon, son of David, king of Israel.

*Solomon was the son of King David, and the third king of
Israel.He reigned during Israel's Golden Age. When God
said he would give him whatever he wanted, Solomon
asked for an understanding mind. Pleased with his request,
God not only made him wise but gave him power and great riches.*

1: 2-6 The purpose of these Proverbs is to teach wisdom, give
instruction and perceive words of understanding. 3To receive
instruction in discipline, good conduct and doing what is right, just
and fair.4 To receive the instruction of wisdom. To the young man
they will give knowledge and purpose. 5 A wise man will hear and
increase wisdom. And let those who understand receive wise counsel,
6by exploring the high depth of meaning in these words of the wise
and their riddles.

(1:6) Riddles are thought provoking questions

1:7 Fear of the Lord is the beginning of knowledge. But fools despise
wisdom and instruction.

*Solomon called the person, who is closed to anything new,
resents discipline and refuses to learn, a fool. Don't be a
fool, be open to the advice of others, from the leaders of*

> *the church, and those who know you well and can give*
> *you meaningful insight and counsel. Be open to learn from others.*

1:8-9 Listen, my son, to what your father teaches you. And do not forsake the law of your mother. 9What you learn from them will be a graceful ornament on your head.

> *Children learn morals, values and priorities by observing*
> *how their parents act and react. If parents show reverence*
> *for God, children will grab on to these attitudes. Teach them*
> *right living by making worship an important part in your life.*

1:10-19 My son, if sinners entice you, turn your back on them! 11They may say, "Come and join us. Let's hide and kill someone. Let's ambush the innocent. 12 Let's swallow them alive as the grave swallows its victims. Though they are in the prime of their life, they will go down into the pit of death. 13 And the loot we'll get! We'll fill our houses with all kinds of things! 14 Come on, throw in your lot with us; we'll split our loot with you!" 15 Don't go along with them, my son! Stay far away from their paths. 16 They rush to commit crimes. They hurry to commit murder. 17 When a bird sees a trap being set, it stays away. 18 But not these people! They set an ambush for themselves; they booby-trap their own lives! 19 Such is the fate of all who are greedy for gain. It ends up robbing them of life.

> *Sin is enticing, as it offers a quick path to prosperity and*
> *makes us feel like we're part of the crowd. Even when attractive,*
> *sin is deadly. We need to learn to make the right choices, not on*
> *the foundation of flashy appeal or short range pleasures, but in*
> *view of long-term effects. Sometimes this means staying clear of*
> *those who want to pressure us into things that we know are wrong.*
> *We cannot befriend sin and expect our lives to go on unaffected.*

1:20-28 Lady Wisdom goes out in the streets and shouts, she cries out in the public square. At the openings of the gates of the city, she speaks her words: 22 "Simpletons, how long will you wallow in ignorance? How long will you mockers relish your mocking? And how long will you fools refuse to learn? 23 Come here and listen to me! I can revise your life. I'm ready to pour out my spirit on you and make my wise words known to you.24 I have called you many times and you refused to come. I have stretched out my hand to you, but you paid no attention. 25 You laughed at my counsel and made a joke of my advice. 26 So I, too, will laugh when you are in trouble! I will mock you when your troubles come, 27 When your terror comes like a storm, and your destruction like a whirlwind, and anguish and distress overwhelm you, 28 You'll call for me, but don't expect an answer. No matter how hard you look, you won't find me.

REJECTING ADVICE

1:29-33 For they hated knowledge and chose not to fear the Lord. 30 They rejected my advice and paid no attention when I corrected them. 31 That is why they must eat the bitter fruit of living their own way. They must experience the full terror of the path they have chosen. 32 For they are simpletons who turn away from me and turn to death. They are fools and their own complacency will destroy them. 33 But all who listen to me will live in peace and safety, unafraid of harm.

*To receive God's advice, we must be willing to listen
and not let pride stand in our way. We should not
think more highly of our own wisdom and desires, than
of God's. If we think we know better than, or have no
need of God's direction, we have fallen into foolish
and disaster-filled pride. People with this type of thinking
will create problems for themselves that will destroy them.
Do not ignore God's advice, even if it's painful for your
present. It will protect you from far greater pain
in the future.*

What lessons did you learn from this chapter?

_____

_____

_____

_____

_____

_____

_____

Chapter 2

Value of Wisdom

2:1-6 My son, listen to my words, and treasure my instructions. 2 Tune your ears to a world of wisdom, and set your heart on a life of understanding. 3 Cry out for insight and understanding. 4 Search for them as you would lost money or hidden treasure. 5 Then you will understand the fear the Lord, and you will find the knowledge of God. 6 For the Lord gives wisdom! From his mouth comes knowledge and understanding.

> *(2:3-6)There is two ways wisdom comes: It is a God-given gift and also from a persistent search. The starting point for wisdom is God and his Word, which is the source of "knowledge & understanding". The pathway to wisdom is not easy, but when we are on the path, we discover that true wisdom is God's. He will guide us and reward our "determined" search.*

2:7-11 He grants good sense to the righteous and he protects those who walk with integrity, 8 Guarding the paths of justice and protecting those who are faithful to him. 9Then you will understand righteousness and justice, and you will know how to find the right path every time. 10 For wisdom will enter your heart and knowledge will be pleasant to your soul. 11 Wise planning will watch over you; understanding will keep you safe.

> *(2:9-10) We gain wisdom through a continual process of growing. Trust & honor God. Realize that the Bible reveals God's wisdom to us, and that we must make a life-long series of right choices and earnestly avoid moral downfalls. When we make sinful choices & mistakes, we need to learn from*

*our errors and bounce back. We don't develop all aspects
of wisdom at once. For instance; some people have more
insight than discretion, while others have more knowledge
than common sense. But we can pray for all aspects of
wisdom and take the steps to develop them in our lives.*

2:12-19 Wisdom will deliver you from the way of evil, from men with corrupt speech. 13 From those who leave the path of righteousness, to walk in the ways of darkness. 14 They rejoice in doing evil, and delight in the sinful behavior of the wicked. 15 Whose paths are crooked, and whose ways are wrong. 16 Wisdom will protect you from the immoral woman, from the seductress who flatters with her words. 17 She forsakes her husband and forgets the covenant she made before God. 18 Entering her house leads to death; the road leads straight to hell. 19 Those who visit her are doomed; they never regain the path to life.

*(2:16-17) Two of the hardest sins to resist are pride and sexual
immortality. Both of these sins are seductive. While
pride says, I deserve it, sexual desire says, I need it.
Together, the appeal is deadly. Solomon says, we can
only overcome them by relying on God's strength.
Pride appeals to the empty head, sexual enticement
appeals to the empty heart. We can fill our heads with
wisdom and our hearts with love, by looking to God.
Ask him for strength when you face these temptations.*

2:20-22 So, join the company of the good men and women; keep your feet on the path of the righteous. 21 For the upright will live in the land, and the blameless will remain in it. 22 But the wicked will be removed from the land, and the unfaithful will be destroyed.

What lessons did you learn from this chapter?

_____

_____

_____

_____

_____

_____

_____

Chapter 3

GUIDANCE FOR THE YOUNG

3:1-3 My child, never forget all I've taught you; take to heart my commands, 2 For they will give you a long, peaceful life. 3 Never let loyalty and kindness get away from you. Bind them around your neck; write them on the tablet of your heart.

> *(3:3)Kindness & loyalty are important character qualities,*
> *as both involve actions as well as attitudes. A loyal*
> *person works for justice for others. Our life reveals*
> *whether we are truly kind & loyal.*
> *Do your actions measure up to your attitudes?*

3:4-6 Then in God's eyes and the eyes of the people, you will earn the reputation for living well. 5 Trust in the Lord with all your heart; and lean not on your own understanding. 6.In all your ways acknowledge him, and he shall direct your paths.

> *(3:5-6) God knows what's best for us. He is a better judge*
> *of what we want than we are. We must trust him*
> *completely in every choice we make. We should be*
> *willing to listen to and be connected by God's Word*
> *and by wise counselors. Bring all of your decisions*
> *to God in prayer, use the Bible as a guide, then follow*
> *his leading. He will not only guide you, but protect you*
> *as well, because you will be working to accomplish his*
> *purpose.*

3:7-10 Don't be wise in your own eyes; fear the Lord and run from evil. 8 Your body will glow with health; and your bones will vibrate with life.9Honor the Lord with your possessions and with the firstfruits of all your increase. 10 So your barns will be filled with plenty and your vats will overflow with new wine.

> *(3:9-10) People tend to give God what's left, after the bills are paid, and if they can afford to give anything, they do so. They may be sincere and give willingly, but they aren't obeying what God is saying. "The firstfruits of your income", meaning the first part of your income, even before the bills are paid. This demonstrates that God has first place in our lives, not our possessions, and that all our resources belong to him, and we are only managers. By giving to God helps us to conquer greed, helps us manage God's resources properly, and opens us up to receive God's special blessings.*

3:11-12 My son, do not ignore it when the Lord chastises you, and don't be discouraged when he corrects you. 12 For the Lord corrects those he loves, just as a father corrects a child in whom he delights.

> *(3:11-12)Discipline is defined as, "to teach and to train". To some people discipline sounds negative because some disciplinarians are not loving. But God "is" the source of all love. He doesn't punish us because he gets pleasure from it, but because he is concerned about our development. He knows that we must learn the difference between right and wrong in order to become morally strong & good. It may not be easy to see when God has been disciplining us until we look back on the situation later.*

3:13-17 Happy is the man who finds wisdom, and the man who gains understanding. 14 For the profit of wisdom is better than money in the bank; and her wages are better than gold. 15 Wisdom is more precious than rubies; And all the things you may desire cannot compare with her. 16 She offers you life in her right hand and riches and honor in her left. 17 She will guide you down pleasant paths; and all her paths are peace.

> *(3:16-17) Proverbs contains many strong statements about the benefits of wisdom, including long life, wealth, honor and peace. If you are not experiencing these things, it does not mean you lack wisdom. These statements are general principals, not guarantees.*

*Only in a perfect world would wise behavior lead
to these benefits. In our troubled world, living wisely
can result in obvious blessings, but not always.
When sin intervenes some blessings may be delayed
until Jesus returns to establish his eternal kingdom.
Either way, we can be sure that wisdom will lead
to blessings.*

3:18-26 Wisdom is a tree of life to those who embrace her; and happy are all who retain her. 19 By wisdom, the Lord founded the earth; by understanding, he established the heavens. 20 By his knowledge, the deep fountains of the earth broke open, and the dew dropped from the clouds. 21 My son, do not lose sight of these, guard clear-thinking and common sense with your life. 22 And they will keep your soul alive and well. 23 Then you will walk on your way safely, and your feet will not stumble. 24 When you lie down, you will not have any fear and your dreams will be pleasant. 25 You need not be afraid of terror or of the destruction of the wicked when it comes. 26 For the Lord will be your protector; he will keep your foot from being caught in a trap.

3:27-28 Do not withhold good from those whom it is due, when it's in your power to help them. 28 If you can help your neighbor now, don't say, "Go and come back tomorrow, and then I will help you".

*(3:27-28) Withholding good is not fair. Not repaying a loan or returning a
borrowed item is a form of stealing and it destroys trust and creates
resentment in the other person. Be as anxious to do good as
you are to have good done to you.*

3:29-35 Do not plot evil against your neighbors, for they trust you. 30 Don't make accusations against a man without cause. 31 Do not envy the oppressor, do not copy their ways. 32 Such people are an abomination to God, but he offers his friendship to the upright. 33 The curse of the Lord is on the house of the wicked, but his blessing is on the home of the just. 34 The Lord mocks mockers, but he gives his grace to the humble. 35 The wise will inherit honor, but the fool will be put to shame.

*(3:29-35) Plotting evil and making false accusations against
a person is a sin and is cause to lose their trust and
respect. Never envy an evildoer, nor do as they do.*

> *God despises such people and they will answer before*
> *him. But God remains close to those who honor him*
> *and who strive to be upright. The wise will inherit God's*
> *honor, but a fool will eventually be exposed.*

What lessons did you learn from this chapter?

_____

_____

_____

_____

_____

_____

_____

Chapter 4
SECURITY IN WISDOM

4:1-4 Hear, my children, listen to your father's instruction, pay attention and grow wise, 2 for I am giving you good doctrine. Do not turn away from my teaching. 3 When I was my father's son, loved tenderly by my mother and an only child. 4 My father told me, "let your heart retain my words and follow my instructions and you will live."

One of the greatest responsibilities of a parent is to encourage their children to become wise. David, Solomon's father, encouraged him when he was young, to seek wisdom. That encouragement may have persuaded Solomon to ask God for an understanding mind above all else. Wisdom should be passed on from generation to generation, from parents to children. All wisdom comes from God and parents can only urge their children to turn to him. If you have never been taught this way, you can learn wisdom from the Scriptures and pass them on to your own children.

4:5-7 Learn to be wise and develop good judgment. Don't forget or turn away from these words. 6 Never turn away from wisdom and she will protect you. Love her and you will be guarded. 7 Gaining wisdom is the most important thing you can do! And also, get good judgment.

Go after wisdom if you want to gain it. It takes determination to not abandon the search once it's begun, no matter how rough the road may become. It is a daily process of choosing between the path of the wicked or the righteous. There is nothing more important or more valuable. Solomon chose wisdom above all else, as he was taught as a child, and we too should make God's wisdom our first choice.

> *We can ask God for wisdom today through prayer, and*
> *we are assured that God will grant it to us.*

4:8-12 If you delight in wisdom, she will fill you with joy; if you embrace her, she will reward you. 9 She will place on your head an ornament of grace; a beautiful crown she will deliver to you. 10 My son, listen to me and do as I say and the years of your life will be many. 11 I will teach you the ways of wisdom; I will lead you on straight paths. 12 If you live your life guided by wisdom, as you run, you will not stumble.

> *Passing on wisdom to your children is the greatest*
> *love you can give to them, as you help guide them*
> *into a life of righteousness. Wisdom will keep their*
> *paths straight as they go through the daily struggles*
> *in life and their ways will be pleasing to our*
> *Heavenly Father.*

4:13-17 Don't forsake my instructions and carry them out. Guard them and they will lead you to a life of fulfillment. 14 Do not do as the wicked ones do or follow in the paths of the evildoers. 15 Avoid them, turn away and go elsewhere, 16 for evildoers cannot rest until they have accomplished their evil doings for the day. They cannot sleep until they have caused someone to fall. 17 They eat wickedness and drink violence!

> *(4:14-17) Even the best of friends can make you stumble. It is*
> *difficult for some to accept that friends and acquaintances*
> *could persuade them to do wrong. Young people want to*
> *be accepted and they may never want to confront or criticize*
> *a friend for wrong actions or plans. We should be accepting*
> *of others but we need to be conscience of human behavior.*
> *If you feel yourself being heavily influenced, be cautious and*
> *don't let anyone cause you to fall into sin.*

4:18-27 The path of the righteous is like the light of dawn, which shines brighter and brighter until it reaches the full light of day. 19 The way of the wicked is like total darkness; they have no idea what they are stumbling over. 20 My son, listen carefully; pay attention to what I say. 21 Don't let my words escape your sight; keep them close to your heart. 22 Learn the meaning of these words and live. Your body and soul will be bursting with health. 23 Above all else, protect your heart, for from it flows the springs of life. 24 Avoid all talk of perversion, stay far from corrupted speech. 25 Look straight and set your eyes on what lies before you. 26 Plan out a path not crooked for your feet, then hold firm on the path and keep safe. 27 Don't sway; keep yourself from following evil.

> *(4:23-27) Our heart, to a great extent, dictates how we live, because we always want to do what we enjoy. Solomon tells us to guard our hearts and concentrate on the desires that will keep us on the right path. Put boundaries on your desires, focus on straight ahead and sternly fix your eyes on your goal and don't take detours that lead to sin.*

What lessons did you learn from this chapter?

_____

_____

_____

_____

_____

_____

_____

Chapter 5
THE IMMORAL WOMAN

5:1-8 My friend, pay close attention and listen carefully to my wise counsel. 2 Then you will acquire a taste for good sense; what I tell you will teach you to store up knowledge. 3 The lips of the immoral woman are oh so sweet; her soft words are as smooth as oil. 4 But it won't be long before she's gravel in your mouth, bitter as poison, a pain in your gut and a wound in your heart. 5 She's dancing down the path to death; she's headed straight to Hell and taking you with her. 6 For she has no clue about Real Life, about who she is or where she is going. 7 So, my friend, listen closely; don't treat my words lightly or stray from what I'm about to say: 8 Keep your distance from such a woman, don't go near the door of her house.

> *(5:3-8) A prostitute is the "immoral woman" and Proverbs points out many warnings against this kind of sex for many reasons. First, an immoral woman's charm is a temptation to do wrong or to cause you to sway from the pursuit of wisdom. Second, sexual immortality is dangerous. It destroys a person's ability to love, it erodes family life and it belittles human beings, turning them into objects. It can result in unwanted children or lead to disease. Thirdly, it is against God's law. The most valuable advice is to turn away and even avoid conversation with such a person.*

5:9-14 You don't want to squander your life and hand over to hardhearted people everything you achieved in life. 10 Why should you allow strangers to obtain your wealth and take advantage of you? Why be exploited by those who care nothing for you? 11 You don't want to end your life full of regrets, nothing but sin and bones, 12 saying, "Oh why didn't I do what they told me? Why did I reject a disciplined life?

13 Why didn't I listen to my mentors or take my teachers seriously? 14 My life is ruined! And now I must face public disgrace."

> *(5:11-13) It will be too late to ask for advice when your life comes to an end. People don't want advice when desire is fully activated, they want satisfaction. The best time to learn the dangers of pursuing forbidden sex, is long before the temptation arises. The resistance to it is easier if the decision has already been made. Preparing for temptation now will help you decide how to act when you face it.*

5:15-23 Drink from your own rain barrel, share your love only with your wife. 16 Or one day you may come home and find your barrel empty and your well polluted. 17 Your barrel is for you and you only, not to be passed around among strangers. 18 Let your wife be a fountain of blessing for you. Enjoy the wife you married as a young man! 19 Lovely as an angel, graceful as a deer. Let her breasts satisfy you always. Don't ever quit taking delight in her body. 20 Why be captivated, my friend, with an immoral woman or embrace the breasts of such a woman? 21 Mark well that the Lord doesn't miss a move you make, he's aware of every step you take. 22 The shadow of your sin will overtake you; they are ropes that catch and bind you. 23 You will die for lack of self-control; your foolish decisions will trap you in a dead-end.

> *(515) :"Drink from your own rain barrel" is an example of faithfulness in marriage, to enjoy the spouse God has given you.*

> *(5:15-21) In contrast to what we read, hear and see today, couples should look to each other for life-long satisfaction and companionship. When marriage becomes dull many temptations entice husbands and wives to leave their spouses and find pleasures and excitement elsewhere. Only in this covenant relationship of marriage, that God designed and sanctified, can we find real love and fulfillment. Don't be blinded by the illusion that greener pastures are somewhere else. Instead, delight in your spouse as you give yourselves to God and to each other.*

> *(5:18-20)Sex is a gift God gives to married people for their enjoyment and real happiness*

*comes when we find pleasure in the spouse he has
given us and to commit ourselves to meeting each other's
needs. The real danger is when we carelessly
pursue sexual pleasure without God's blessing.*

What lesson did you learn from this chapter?

_____

_____

_____

_____

_____

_____

_____

Chapter 6
Daily Life Lessons

6:1-5 My son, if you co-sign a loan for your friend or guarantee the debt of a stranger, 2 you have snared yourself by your agreement, you are caught by the words of your mouth. 3 So do this, my son, and get out of it if you can. For you have put yourself at the mercy of your friend. Go and humble yourself; plead with your friend to have your named erased. 4 Don't sleep on it, do it now! Don't slumber until you do. 5 Deliver yourself like a deer from the hand of the hunter, like a bird from the trap of the fowler.

> *These verses are not against generosity, but against acting irresponsibly and overextending your financial resources. It is important to balance oneself between good stewardship and generosity. We should help the needy, but we need to act responsibly, so not to bring a burden on ourselves or our family.*

The Folly of Habitual Laziness

6:6-11 You lazy fool, look at the ant and take a lesson. Learn their ways and be wise. 7 They have no captain, no overseer or ruler, 8 but they work hard all summer and gather food in the harvest. 9 How long will you lazybones slumber? When will you wake from your sleep? 10 A little sleep, a little slumber, a little folding of the hands to sleep, 11 And poverty will come on you like a prowler, it will steal your needs like an armed bandit.

> *These passages warn us about laziness, of sleeping instead of working. We do need rest but we should not be resting when we should be working. The ant is an example of working diligently, to produce our harvest. Then we will have our resources, and see our hard work has paid off and we can now enjoy our rest.*

The Wicked Person

6:12-19 A worthless person, the wicked man, is directed away from what is right or good. 13They are liars, winking with their eyes, shuffling with their feet and pointing with their fingers. 14 Perversity is in their hearts. They continually plot evil and stir up trouble. 15 But severe affliction will come upon them suddenly. They shall be broken beyond all hope of healing. 16-19 Here are six things God hates, and one more he detests:

- Arrogant eyes
- A lying tongue
- Hands that kill the innocent
- A heart that plots evil
- Feet that race down a wicked path
- A witness that speaks lies
- A person that causes trouble in the family

6:20-23 My son, keep your father's commands and do not forsake your mother's teachings. 21 Bind their words into your heart; Tie them around your neck. 22 When you walk, their counsel will lead you. When you sleep, they will protect you. And when you awake, they will advise you. 23 For these commands are a lamp to light the path ahead of you. Moral discipline is the way to life.

> *Although we may have grown older and more independent,*
> *we should take care not to reject our parent's advice. If you're*
> *faced with a problem or struggling with a decision, go to your*
> *parents or other older persons that know you well. Their years*
> *of experience just might be the wisdom you're looking for.*

Avoiding the Adulteress

6:25-35 Don't lust after her beauty in your heart, nor let her lure you with her bedroom eyes. 26 A prostitute will bring you to poverty, and sleeping with another's wife may cost you your own life. 27 Can anyone hold fire in their lap and not be burned? 28 Can he walk on hot coals and his feet not blister? 29 Same goes for the man who sleeps with his neighbor's wife. He will not go unpunished. 30 People may not despise a thief if he steals because he is starving, 31 But if he is caught he must pay back seven times the amount that was stolen, even if it means selling everything in his house to do so. 32 But the person who commits adultery is a fool. He lacks understanding and destroys his own soul. 33 Wounds and dishonor he will get. His shame will not be wiped away. 34 For jealousy will be the husband's fury, and he will not show any mercy in his day of vengeance. 35 There is no compensation, nor any amount of gifts that will appease him.

> *With the sin of adultery, somebody always gets hurt. Spouses are crushed and children are affected. Long-term emotional troubles could result from the devastation it causes. If the woman should get pregnant, it may result in an abortion, resulting in another sin. With sexual sin, partners may lose the ability to fulfill commitments, to trust and to be totally open with another person. God's law warns us against destroying ourselves through immoral actions.*

What lessons did you learn from this chapter?

_____

_____

_____

_____

_____

_____

_____

_____

Chapter 7
More Warnings About Immoral Women

7:1-5 Keep my words, my son, and treasure my commands. 2 Obey these commands and live, and guard them as your most precious possession. 3 Bind them on your fingers as a reminder; write them on the tablet of your heart. 4 Say to wisdom, "You are my sister", and make insight your closest relative. 5 And let them keep you from the immoral woman, from the seductress that flatters with her words.

Proverbs talks many times about the immoral woman, and how getting involved with her could lead to many troubles. Taking advice from your father or other older adults that know you well, is for your own benefit. Their years of experience shouldn't be ignored, as they are only guiding us to a path that will not lead us to dangers or troubles.

The Promiscuous Woman
7:6-12 From the window of my house I looked out through the shutters, 7 I spotted a mindless young man who lacked common sense. 8 He was passing along the street near her corner, and he took the path to her house. 9 It was dusk, the day was fading and the dark of night was setting in. 10 And there a woman met him, dressed to seduce and with a crafty heart. 11 She was the loud, rebellious type who never stays at home. 12 Often she can be seen in the streets and at the markets, hanging out at every corner.

Even though this advice is mainly directed towards young men, young women should also give careful attention as well. The person who has no purpose in life is mindless. Without aim or direction, life is unsettled, and vulnerable to many temptations.

7:13-23 She put her arms around him and kissed him, and with a shameless look she said, 14 I've got all the makings for a feast; Today I made my offerings and my vows are all paid. 15 So I came out to meet you, persistently to seek your face, and I have found you. 16 I have spread my bed with colored sheets from the finest Egyptian linens. 17 I have perfumed my bed with aromatic perfumes, aloes, and cinnamon. 18 Come, let us take our fill of love until morning. Let us delight ourselves with each other's caresses. 19 For my husband is not at home. He has gone on a long journey. 20 He has taken a bag of money with him and won't be back for at least a month. 21 With her pretty speech and flattering, she seduces him. 22 Immediately he followed after her, like an ox going to the slaughter or like a dog on a leash. 23 Like a bird flying into a net, not knowing it would cost him his life.

> *Even though the young man doesn't know where he's going, the woman knows where she wants him. Look at her strategies: She is dressed seductively; her approach is bold; she invites him to her house; she persuades him with smooth talk; she traps him. To battle these temptations, your life has to be full of God's Word and wisdom. Be observant of the strategies of temptation and run away, fast!*

7:24-27 Therefore, listen to me, my sons, and pay attention to my words. 25 Don't fool around with a woman like that; don't even stroll into her neighborhood. 26 Countless victims come under her spell; she has been the ruin of many men. 27 Her house is the way to hell. Her bedroom is the den of death.

> *Take the steps to avoid sexual sins. First, guard your mind. Avoid thinking and fantasizing. Don't read books or look at pictures that can arouse the wrong desires. Also, you should keep away from friends or settings that tempt you to sin. In this day and age, the internet is easy access to pornography and adult sites that can easily tempt us. Don't think only of the moment, think ahead. Today's thrill could lead you to tomorrow's sin.*

What lessons did you learn from this chapter?

_____

_____

_____

_____

_____

_____

_____

Chapter 8
LADY WISDOM CALLS OUT

8:1-11 Do you hear Lady Wisdom calling? And understanding lifting up her voice? 2 She takes her stand at the busiest intersection. 3 She cries out by the gates, at the entrance of the city. 4 "You, I'm talking to all of you! I am raising my voice to all people. 5 Listen, you foolish ones, learn good sense! Let me give your understanding. 6 Listen to me! I speak of excellent things; from my lips come right things. 7 For I speak the truth, wickedness is not in my vocabulary. 8 All my words are wholesome and good; nothing crooked or twisted in it. 9 These words are plain to those with understanding, and clear to those who want to learn. 10 Choose my instructions over chasing after money and knowledge over a lucrative career. 11 For wisdom is better than all the trappings of wealth; and all the things you may desire cannot compare to her.

> *Wisdom should affect every aspect of our life, from beginning to end. God approves of those who listen to Wisdom's counsel. Many people chase after money and careers, but it says here that having wisdom is much better to possess than money or position. Open all corners of your life to God's direction and guidance.*

8:12-21 I, Wisdom, dwell together with good judgment. Knowledge and discernment live next door. 13 All who fear the Lord hate evil. They hate pride, arrogance, corruption and perverted speech. 14 Good counsel and common sense are my characteristics. I am understanding and have the strength to live it out. 15 Because of me, kings reign and rulers legislate fair laws. 16 Rulers lead with my help and the noble man make righteous judgments. 17 I love those who love me, and those who seek me diligently will find me. 18 Unending riches, honor and justice are mine to distribute. 19 My benefits are better than a big salary; and my revenue better than the purest gold. 20 I walk in righteousness, in the paths of justice. 21 For those who love me inherit wealth, for I fill their treasuries.

> *The more a person fears and respects God, the more he will hate evil. Love for both God and sin cannot coexist. Holding on to secret sins means you are tolerating evil inside yourself. Make a clean break from sin by first confessing them to God, then by committing yourself completely to him. These verses also talk about listening to good counsel, having common sense and diligently seeking wisdom. Successful leaders are led by wisdom and not by the benefits. The benefits of wisdom are worth more than any amount of money and for those who love wisdom, the benefits far exceed what we could ever imagine.*

8:22-31 The Lord sovereignly formed me, before he created anything else. 23 I was brought into being a long time ago, even before the earth began. 24 I was born before the oceans, before the springs and rivers and lakes. 25 Before the mountains were formed and the hills took shape. 26 Before he had made the fields of the earth, or the first dust of the world. 27 When he prepared the heavens, I was there, and also when he drew a boundary for the sea. 28 I was there when he established the clouds above and when he strengthened the deep fountains of the earth. 29 When he assigned the limits to the sea, so the waters would not spread beyond their boundaries. And when he marked out the foundations of the earth, 30 I was beside him as a master craftsman; and I was his daily delight, rejoicing always before him. 31 I rejoiced with what he created, and cheerfully celebrated the human family.

> *Wisdom reveals herself as preceding all creation, and is the foundation on which all life is built. Here, Jesus, the Son of Man, was engaged in the creation of the world and eventually became the Savior of the world. Who better to save us, than the one who created us?*

8:32-36 Now therefore, listen to me, my children, for blessed are those who follow my ways. 33 Hear my instruction and be wise, and do not ignore it. 34 Blessed are those who listen to me, watching for me daily at my gates, and waiting for me outside my door. 35 For whoever finds me finds life and obtains approval from the Lord. 36 But if you wrong me, you damage your very soul; when you reject me, you're flirting with death.

> *Here, wisdom is speaking directly to us, telling us to be persistent in our quest to find her. When we earnestly seek wisdom, we gain God's approval. But if we ignore the instruction to find it, we could lose something more valuable. Our soul!*

What lessons did you learn from this chapter?

_____

_____

_____

_____

_____

_____

_____

Chapter 9
THE WAY OF WISDOM

9:1-5 Wisdom has built her house and roughly shaped out her seven pillars. 2 The banquet meal is ready to be served, the wines are mixed and the table is set. 3 She has sent out her maidens, she cries out from the heights overlooking the city, inviting everyone to come. 4 Come to my house, she urges the simple. To those who lack understanding, she says, 5 Come, eat my food and drink the wine I have mixed. 6 Turn your back on foolishness and live; walk up the street to a life with meaning.

> *The seven pillars are figurative. In the Bible, the number seven represents perfection and completeness. Wisdom lacks nothing, it is perfect and complete. Many may intend to go to a banquet, as described in this chapter, but they never make it because they get sidetracked by activities that seem more important at the time. Don't allow anything to become more important than your search for God's Wisdom.*

9:7-12 Anyone who reasons with an arrogant cynic, will get slapped in the face. And anyone who scolds a wicked man will get hurt. 8 So don't waste your time reprimanding mockers, they will hate you for it. But if you correct those who care about life, they will love you for it. 9 Give instruction to a wise man and he will be wiser. Tell good people what you know and they'll profit from it. 10 The fear of the Lord is the beginning of Wisdom. Knowledge of the Holy One results in understanding. 11 For by wisdom, your days will be multiplied and years will be added to your life. 12 Live wisely and wisdom will saturate your life; mock life and life will mock you.

> *You can tell if you're a mocker or a wise person by the*

> *way you respond to criticism. Listen to what is being*
> *said, instead of replying with a quick put-down or a*
> *clever come back when criticized. The path to wisdom*
> *is learning from your critics. Wisdom begins with know-*
> *ing God. Do you really want to be wise? Get to know God*
> *better. Not just by having the facts about him, but by*
> *having a personal relationship with him.*

The Way of Folly

9:13-18 Then there's a woman named Folly; brazen, empty-headed, frivolous. 14 She sits on the front porch of her house on Main Street. 15 And as men walk by, minding their own business, she calls out; 16 "Whoever is simple, come home with me". To those without good judgment she says, 17 "Stolen water is refreshing and no one will ever know. I'll give you the time of your life". 18 But they don't know about all the skeletons in her closet, that all her guests end up in hell.

> *There is something attractive about wickedness and sinful*
> *behavior seems more exciting than Christian life. That's*
> *why many put aside the thought of Wisdom's lavish banquet*
> *in order to eat the stolen food of Folly. But remember, sin is*
> *dangerous. Before falling into the folly, remember what*
> *happened to those who have already fell.*

What lessons did you learn from this chapter?

_____

_____

_____

_____

_____

_____

_____

Chapter 10
WISE SAYINGS OF SOLOMON

The Proverbs of Solomon:
10:1-3 A wise son makes a glad father, but a foolish son brings grief to a mother. 2 Ill-gotten gain has no lasting value, but an honest life delivers us from death. 3 God won't starve an honest soul, but he refuses to satisfy the appetites of the wicked.

> *Some people can bring unhappiness on themselves by choosing ill-gotten gain. Craving satisfaction, they may do something that ruins their chances of ever achieving happiness. Gambling is one perfect example of this. Craving the satisfaction of the "big win" people get addicted. They find themselves in poverty and all chances of happiness destroyed. God's principals for right living bring lasting happiness, as they guide us into right-behavior in spite of our ever changing feelings.*

> *(10:3) Proverbs has many verses contrasting the righteous person with the wicked. These statements are general truths that are intended to communicate the life of a person who seeks God is better in the long-run than the life of the wicked person, whose life leads to ruin. A proverb like this assumes a government that cares for the poor and needy, not a corrupt government that often alters the plans of godly men and women.*

10:4-5 Lazy people are soon poor, but hard work brings wealth. 5 He who works hard in the summer is a wise son; but he who sleeps during harvest time, is a son who causes shame.

> *Everyday has opportunities for us to grow, to serve and be productive, yet it is easy to let life slip away from us. Don't give in to being lazy. Don't waste away the hours*

> *meant for productive work. Time is God's gift and we*
> *should take every opportunity to live diligently for Him.*

10:6-10 The righteous are showered with blessings; but the mouth of the wicked speaks harshly. 7 The memories of a godly person are happy memories; while the name of a wicked person rots away. 8 A wise heart takes instruction; but a fool who talks pointlessly will fall flat on his face. 9 He who lives honestly, lives secure; but he who follows crooked paths will be exposed. 10 He who winks at wrong, causes trouble; but an open, face-to-face meeting, promotes peace.

10:11-14 The mouth of a good person is a deep, life-giving well; but the mouth of the wicked speaks harshly. 12 Hatred starts fights, but love covers all offenses. 13 Wisdom is found on the lips of those with understanding; but punishment is for fools who do not possess understanding. 14 Wise people accumulate knowledge; but the pointless talk of a fool invites trouble.

> *Many passages in Proverbs point out the words that*
> *come from our lips can either be wise or foolish words.*
> *We can usually tell a lot about someone by the manner*
> *in which they speak. Kind words soothe, while harsh words*
> *can stir trouble. When a person seeks wise advice ,they will*
> *ask a person who possesses understanding, rather than the*
> *person who speaks foolishly. Which category do you fall in?*

10:15-18 The rich man's wealth is his fortress; the poverty of the poor is their misery. 16 The wages of the righteous enhance their lives; but an evil person ends up with nothing but sin. 17 Those who accept instruction are on the pathway to life; but those who refuse correction, will lead others astray. 18 Whoever hides hatred is a liar; and fools openly spread slander.

> *You may become a liar or a fool if you have hatred*
> *for another person. When you hide your hatred,*
> *you end up lying and if you slander another person*
> *and are proven wrong, you are a fool. If you're*
> *concealing hateful feelings, admit them to God and*
> *ask him to change your heart. Most times hatred is*
> *hard to let go of, but God wants us to love and he will*

*give you the help to overcome the hate and replace it
with love.*

10:19-24 The more you talk, the less is truth; be wise and measure your words. 20 The words of the righteous is like the finest silver; but the heart of the wicked is worthless. 21 The talk of a good person is beneficial to many; but fools die for their lack of wisdom. 22 The blessings of the Lord makes a person rich, and he adds no sorrow with it. 23 Mischief is fun for a fool; but a mindful person relishes wisdom. 24 Whatever the wicked person fears will come true; and so will the hopes of the righteous.

> *Words from a good person are valuable. If you seek
> advice, don't seek it from someone who will only tell
> you what you want to hear, that will do no good.
> Instead, turn to someone who will speak the truth,
> even if it hurts. It's for our own benefit.*

> *(10:24) People who don't believe in God usually
> fear death, but believers desire to be with God
> in eternity. You can have either your fears or
> your hopes come true, by making a choice. A
> choice to live your own way and reject God, or
> by accepting God and following him.*

10:25-32 When the cyclone strikes, the wicked are whirled away; but the righteous aren't even fazed. 26 A lazy employee will give you nothing but trouble; it's like vinegar in your mouth or smoke in your eyes. 27 If you fear the Lord your life will be prolonged; but the years of the wicked will be cut short. 28 The hopes of the godly ends in celebration; but the expectations of the wicked will suffer destruction. 29 The way of the Lord gives strength to the upright; but destruction will come to the wicked. 30 The godly will never be removed; but the wicked will not inhibit the earth. 31 A righteous person gives good advice; but a foul-mouth is like a stagnant swamp. 32 The righteous speak words that cleanse the air; the wicked speak words that pollute it.

What lessons did you learn from this chapter?

_____

_____

_____

_____

_____

_____

_____

Chapter 11
WITHOUT GOOD DIRECTION, PEOPLE LOSE THEIR WAY

11:1-4 The Lord hates cheating in the marketplace, but he delights in honesty. 2 The stuck-up fall flat on their faces, but those who are humble comes wisdom. 3 An honest person's integrity keeps them on track, but the dishonesty of the unfaithful brings them to ruin. 4 Riches will be no help to you on the Day of Judgment, but living righteous will deliver you from death.

> *We've all heard people say, "you can't take it with you"*
> *All of us will leave this world just as we came in, with*
> *nothing, and on the Day of Judgment, when we stand*
> *alone before God and give account for all our deeds,*
> *no amount of earthly riches will buy favor with God.*
> *Only our love and obedience to him will count then.*

11:5-9 A moral character makes for smooth traveling, but the wicked will become the victim of their own wickedness. 6 The godliness of good people will rescue them, but the unfaithful will get trapped in their sinful lust. 7 When the wicked person dies, that's it, end of story, no more hope. 8 God rescues a good person from many troubles, but he lets the wicked run straight into it. 9 The evil mouth of a hypocrite will destroy a neighbor; the wise judgment of the godly protects them.

> *God's people are not exempt from struggles or problems,*
> *but if we follow God's lead, he can rescue us from trouble.*
> *The ungodly will eventually fall into their own traps and*
> *when they die, all their hope dies with them. When good*
> *people suffer, it's only temporary and they can be certain*
> *to be rescued from eternal death.*

> *(11:9) What comes out our mouths can either be a weapon*
> *or a tool. Your words make a difference. It is often easier*
> *for our words to be a weapon of destruction, rather than*
> *a building tool. Before you destroy another with your words,*
> *think how it would be if you were the one on the receiving end.*

11:10-14 When it goes well for good people, the town cheers; but when it goes badly for the wicked, the whole town celebrates. 11 A city flourishes when right-living people bless it, but the talk of the wicked tears it apart. 12 People that don't possess wisdom will belittle their neighbor, but the person with good sense will remain silent. 13 A gossip can't be trusted with a secret, but the trustworthy won't violate a confidence. 14 Without good counsel, people lose their way; but with many counselors there is safety.

> *To be a good leader you need good counselors, others*
> *to turn to for advice and direction. One person's views*
> *are limited, as they may not have all the facts and in order*
> *to be a wise leader, whether at home or in your professional*
> *life, you need to seek the counsel of many and be open to*
> *their advice. Consider all the facts, ask God for his help,*
> *then make your decision.*

11:15-19 Whoever guarantees a loan for a stranger is sure to get burned; it is better to refuse than to suffer later.16 A woman with grace gets respect; while a man with no compassion gets rich. 17 When you are kind to others, your soul is strengthened; when you are cruel to others, you are destroying yourself. 18 A wicked man gets rich for the moment; but the righteous man's reward will last. 19 The righteous person's pursuit leads to life; the evil person's pursuits lead to death.

> *The righteous person finds life because they live more*
> *fully each day, while the evil person not only finds*
> *eternal death, but also miss out on real life on earth.*
> *The righteous person usually lives longer when they*
> *live right and they don't fear death because it's God's*
> *gift to them.*

11:20-22 The Lord hates a sinful heart; but he relishes those with sound moral character. 21 Even if all the wicked join together, that won't save them from their due punishment; but those loyal to God will rise up in victory. 22 A beautiful woman who lacks wisdom is like a gold ring in a pig's snout.

> *Physical attraction, without common sense, will*
> *soon wear thin. Taking care of our appearance and*
> *bodies is not wrong, but not everyone who looks good*
> *is pleasant to live with, so we should seek character*
> *strengths that will help us make wise decisions over*
> *physical beauty alone.*

11:23-25 The righteous can look forward to happiness; while the wicked will see the fury of God. 24 Give freely and become more wealthy; but the stingy will end up in poverty. 25 Those who bless others will be abundantly blessed; those who help others will be helped themselves.

> *These passages say we become richer by giving more.*
> *When the world says to hold on to what we have, God*
> *says to give freely, and he will supply us with more so we*
> *can give more. Giving also gives us the right perspective*
> *on what we have. When we realize they are not truly ours,*
> *but given to us by God to be used to help others, we'll find*
> *the freedom from the enslavement of our possessions. We*
> *will also experience the joy of helping others and gaining*
> *the approval of God.*

11:26-29 People will curse those who hold their grain for higher prices; but theybless the one who sells to them in their time of need. 27 The one who seeks good finds good; seek evil and evil will find you. 28 Trust in your money and you will fall; but the righteous will flourish like leaves in the springtime. 29 Those who bring trouble to their own family will inherit the wind; and the fool will be a servant to the wise.

> *Families provide us with acceptance, encouragement,*
> *counsel and guidance. To bring trouble to your family*
> *is foolish because you cut yourself off from all they provide.*
> *In your own family, always strive to communicate well and*
> *to be understanding and loving.*

11:30-31 A good life is like a tree that bears life-giving fruit; and he who save souls are wise. 31 If good people are rewarded here on earth, what's in store for the wicked!

> *A righteous person's sense of purpose, like the shade*
> *of a tree attracts people, attracts others who want to*
> *learn how they too, can find meaning. The first step*
> *in guiding others to God is to gain wisdom yourself.*
> *No one gets away with sin. The godly will be rewarded*
> *for their faith and the wicked will be punished for*
> *their sins. We can't hide from God, even if we think*
> *we won't get caught. He sees it all!*

What lessons did you learn from this chapter?

_____

_____

_____

_____

_____

_____

_____

Chapter 12
IF YOU LOVE LEARNING

12:1-5 If you love instruction, you love knowledge; but it is stupid to hate correction. 2 A good person is the delight of the Lord; but a person of wickedness will be condemned. 3 Wickedness never brings stability; but life rooted in God stands firm. 4 A hearty wife is the crown of her husband; but a wife who causes shame is like a cancer in his bones. 5 The thoughts of the righteous are just; the advice of the wicked is corrupt.

> *If you have no desire to learn, no amount of schooling will do you any good. But if you accept instruction, there is no limit to what you can learn. Be willing to accept correction and discipline and to learn from others. Don't let pride cause you to refuse constructive criticism, or it will be unlikely for you to learn very much.*
> *(12:3) Life rooted in God and stability means to be successful. Real success comes to those who want to do right, and their efforts will stand the test of time. The success of wickedness can come from cheating to pass a course, on a tax return, or the person who ignores family commitments or mistreating co-workers to get ahead in business. But these successes are only temporary and this kind of behavior does not lead to success, only to more evil. True success can only come by way of God's standards.*

12:6-13 The words of the wicked kill; but the words of the righteous save lives. 7 Wicked people fall to pieces and perish; but the homes of the righteous hold together. 8 A person who talks sense is honored; but he with a twisted mind is despised. 9 It is better to be ordinary and work for a living, than to act important and have no food. 10 Good people are good to their animals; but even the mercies of a bad person are cruel. 11 He who works his land will have plenty to eat; but he who idles away his time is a fool. 12 The wicked wrongfully desire the possessions of other evil men; while the righteous work honest for what they have. 13 The gossip of the wicked gets them in trouble; but the righteous will avoid such trouble.

> *The wicked will twist the facts to support what they are saying, but eventually they will be caught in their own lies. Those who always tell the truth don't have to twist their claims. Maybe you're not being honest, if you find that you have to always defend yourself to others.*

12:14-19 Well-spoken words bring satisfaction; and well-done work has many benefits. 15 Fools think they need no counsel; but wise people take advice. 16 Fools are quick-tempered; but the wise remain calm when insulted. 17 The honest witness tells the truth; a dishonest witness tells lies. 18 The tongue of wicked speaks hurtful words; but there is healing in the words of the wise. 19 Truthful words stand the test of time; lies will eventually be exposed.

> *"A gentle answer turns away wrath", so when someone insults you, don't retaliate, instead you should answer slowly and calmly. To achieve a positive result, respond in a positive way.*
> *(12:19) Truth not only applies for today, but also in the future. Truth is connected with God's never changing character and just as the Bible has stood the test of time, because God's Word is truth, so will your words of truth hold up.*

12:20-28 Distortion of the truth is in the heart of those who plot evil; joy is in the heart of those who plan peace. 21 No evil can overwhelm a good person; but the evil have their fill of trouble. 22 Lying lips are a disgrace to the Lord; but he delights in those who keep their word. 23 The wise don't flaunt their knowledge; but fools broadcast their foolishness. 24 Work hard and become a leader; be lazy and become a slave. 25 Worry weighs us down; a cheerful word picks us up. 26 The righteous give good advice to others; the wicked lead them astray. 27 The lazy man does not even cook what he hunted; but persistence is a man's precious possession. 28 A good person's path leads to life; and on this path there is no death.

Although good people are not immune to harm, they are able to see ways out of their problems and move on, while those without God's wisdom, are not equipped to handle their problems.
(12:23) Insecure people feel they need to prove themselves, while wise people have a silent confidence about themselves, and don't have anything to prove. Avoid showing off. Remain modest and people will respect you.
(12:27) The lazy waste their resources, but the persistent make wise use of theirs. Wasting is poor stewardship, so make good use of everything God has given you.

What lessons did you learn from this chapter?

_____

_____

_____

_____

_____

_____

_____

Chapter 13
WALK WITH THE WISE

13:1-5 Children with good sense listen to their parents; foolish children do their own thing. 2 Good people enjoy the positive results of their words; but the souls of the evil feed on violence. 3 Control your tongue and have long life; careless talk can ruin everything. 4 The lazy man desires much, but has nothing; but those who work hard will prosper. 5 A righteous person hates lying; but the repulsive will come to shame.

> *(13:3) The tongue is a powerful weapon. Words from your mouth can cut deep and even destroy. Being self-controlled begins with the tongue, and if you control the words from your mouth, you can control the rest of your body.*

13:6-10 A God-loyal life keeps you on track; but the evil are destroyed by their wickedness. 7 There are those who pretend to be rich, yet have nothing; and some rich pretend to be poor. 8 The rich can be sued for everything they have; but the poor won't even get threatened. 9 The lives of the good are like a brightly lit street; but the lives of the wicked are dark alleys. 10 One's pride leads to arguments; but the wise listen to each other's advice.

> *(13:6) God-loyal living protects your life. Every decision you make to obey the Word of God will keep your life in order, while each decision to disobey his Word will bring confusion and destruction. Obedience brings protection and security.*
>
> *(13:10) Pride is one ingredient in every argument. It causes conflict and divides people. If you find*

> *yourself constantly arguing, take a look at your-*
> *self. Pride just may be the reason. Be open to*
> *receive advice, to ask for help and be willing to*
> *admit your mistakes.*

13:11-16 Wealth from dishonesty is easy come, easy go; but wealth from honest work continues to grow. 12 Disappointment leaves your heart sick; but a sudden good break can turn your life around. 13 Those who refuse advice find trouble; those who respect it, will be rewarded. 14 The teaching of the wise is a fountain of life; it turns one away from the snares of death. 15 Sound thinking makes for a gracious life; but liars walk a rough road. 16 The wise person thinks before they act; but a fool shows off his folly.

> *(13:13) Look at God as "the good parent", who knows*
> *us and loves us and only wants the best for us. Doesn't*
> *it make sense to listen to his instructions and do what he*
> *says? The Bible is his unfailing word to us. It's like an*
> *instruction manual for building something. If we follow*
> *the instructions carefully, we can be assured that whatever*
> *we're putting together is put together correctly.*

13:17-19 A wicked messenger falls into trouble; but a faithful messenger brings health. 18 If you ignore correction, poverty and shame will come upon you; but accepting criticism brings honor. 19 To see a dream come true is sweet to the soul; but a fool will not turn his back on evil to attain this.

> *(13:17) In Solomon's day, messengers were relied upon to*
> *relay information. A reliable messenger was vital.*
> *Wrong information could lead to bloodshed. Vital*
> *information is still important today. If the message*
> *sent was different than the one received, marriages,*
> *businesses and relations could suffer. Choose your*
> *words and don't react until you clearly understand*
> *what the other person means.*

13:20-22 Become wise by walking with the wise; hang out with fools and watch your life fall apart. 21 Trouble follows sinners; while blessings chase the good. 22 A good man leaves an inheritance for his grandchildren; but the wealth of the sinner is passed on to the godly.

*(13:20)Friends accept us and will usually agree with us,
so when we need advice we'll usually go to our
friends first. But our friends are so much like us
that they may not have any answers we haven't
heard already, and may not be able to help us with
a difficult problem. Instead we should seek advice
from older and wiser people, who have experienced
a lot in life. They aren't afraid to speak the truth to us.*

13:23-25 A poor man's farm may produce much crop; but the lack of justice takes it all away. 24 He who withholds discipline from their children cannot love them; to discipline them is to love them. 25 The righteous eat until their bellies are full; but the stomach of the wicked goes hungry.

*The poor are often victimized by an unjust society.
He may have good soil, but crooked laws can rob
him of his own crop. A rich man has the money to
fight these types of injustice, but a poor man is at
another's mercy, but in the end, the justice of God
will prevail.*

*(13:24) The biggest responsibility God gives parents,
is the nurturing and guidance of their children.
Although disciplining a child may not be easy, it is
necessary. Lack of discipline shows a lack of concern
for the development of their character and children
will grow up with little direction in their lives. It's an
act of love to discipline your children, or they will
never know which path is right or wrong.*

What lessons did you learn from this chapter?

_____

_____

_____

_____

_____

_____

_____

Chapter 14
The Way That Leads To Hell

14:1-5 The wise woman builds a lovely home; a foolish woman tears hers down, brick by brick. 2 Those that walk upright have respect for the Lord; but those with immoral ways despise him. 3 The talk of fools is a rod of pride; but the words of the wise keep them safe. 4 Have no oxen and the trough stays clean; but without oxen to plow your field, expect no income. 5 A truthful witness never lies; but a false witness always lies.

> *If a farmer has no oxen to plow his field, he won't have any income. Same goes for our lives. If we avoid people problems by avoiding people, then our life is useless. Live for yourself and your life loses its meaning. Show evidence of your love for God by serving others and sharing your faith.*

14:6-10 Mockers look high and low for wisdom, but never find it; knowledge comes easy to those with understanding. 7 Escape quickly from the company of fools; for you won't find any knowledge there. 8 The wise have the common sense to see what's ahead; but a fool's folly has him blinded. 9 Fools make fun of sin; but the righteous admit it and seek reconciliation. 10 The heart knows its own bitterness; and no other can fully share in its joy.

> *Mockers are people that make fun of and reject instruction or advice. They don't find wisdom because they don't seek it. Applying God's Word to our lives and talking to godly counselors is how we can find wisdom. If the wisdom you seek is hard to find, it may just be your attitude holding you back.*

14:11-13 The house of the wicked will suffer ruin; but the tent of the upright will flourish. 12 There is a path before each of us that seems right; but look again, it leads straight to hell. 13 Laughter may hide a burdened heart; but when the laughter ends, the burden remains.

> *(14:12) The path that "seems right" may give us many choices without much sacrifice, but easy choices should make us look again. The right choice usually requires many sacrifices combined with hard work. Don't be fooled by the "easy road" that seems right, but end in death.*

14:14-19 A mean person will be repaid with meanness; but, a good person is rewarded from above. 15 The gullible believe everything they're told; but those with common sense sift and weigh every word. 16 The wise watch their steps and avoid evil; fools plunge recklessly ahead. 17 A quick-tempered person will do foolish things; and those with wicked intentions are hated. 18 The simple inherit folly; but the wise are crowned with knowledge. 19 Eventually, evil people will bow before good people; the wicked will bow at the gates of the righteous.

14:20-29 A poor man is shunned by all; but the rich man has many friends. 21 It's a sin to ignore a neighbor in need; but those who help the poor will be blessed. 22 Those that plot evil will go astray; but mercy and truth are granted to those who plan good. 23 Hard work pays off; mere talk leads to poverty. 24 The wise accumulate wisdom; fools get more foolish by the day. 25 Souls are saved by a truthful witness; but a deceitful witness speaks lies. 26 Fear of the Lord builds confi- dence; and makes a safe haven for your children. 27 Fear of the Lord is a fountain of life; it offers escape from the snares of death. 28 A good leader has many loyal followers; no followers and his nation is doomed. 29 He who is slow to anger has great understanding; but he who is quick-tempered will make mistakes.

> *(14:29) A quick temper can be like a fire raging out of control, it can burn everyone around us. Anger pushes us into unreasonable decisions that cause bitterness. On the contrary, anger can be a legitimate reaction to an injustice or sin, but we need to look at the cause first. Are you reacting selfishly, or to a situation that you are going to get straight? Pray to God to help you*

*overcome a quick temper and to conquer selfish anger
and to channel those feelings into effective action.*

14:30-35 A sound heart lengthens life; jealousy rots the bones. 31 You insult your Maker when you shun the poor; but those who help the needy, honor God. 32 The wicked are lost in their sin; but the righteous have a safe haven when they die. 33 Wisdom fills an understanding heart; folly fills the fool's heart. 34 Devotion to God makes a country strong; avoiding God weakens it. 35 A leader rejoices in a wise servant; but he despises the servant who causes trouble.

> *(14:31) In the Bible, helping the poor isn't a suggestion,
> it's a command. God is concerned for the poor and He
> insists that those who have wealth or material goods
> should be generous with those who are needy. God
> blessed you so you could bless others.*

What lessons did you learn from this chapter?

_____

_____

_____

_____

_____

_____

Chapter 15
THE EYES OF THE LORD ARE EVERYWHERE

15:1-5 A gentle answer turns away anger; but a harsh word stirs it up. 2 Knowledge flows from the wise like spring water; but the mouth of the fool pours out foolishness. 3 The eyes of the Lord are everywhere; keeping watch over both evil and good. 4 Kind words heal and help; cutting words crush the spirit. 5 A fool despises a parent's instruction; but the wise learn from correction.

> *Raising your voice and shouting harsh words will usually trigger an angry response. By choosing gentle words will turn away anger.*

> *(15:3) God sees everything, the evil actions and the evil intent behind the action. Sometimes we wonder if God even notices all the evil around, but He does care and is active in the world. Even though His work may be unfelt, don't give up. One day evil will be wiped out and the evildoers will be punished and rewards will come to those who do his will.*

15:6-15 The lives of the God-loyal people flourish; but a misspent life is soon bankrupt. 7 Only the wise can give good knowledge; but the lips of a fool cannot do so. 8 Those that pose as being righteous are an abomination to the Lord; but he delights in those with genuine prayers. 9 The ways of the wicked are despised by the Lord; but he loves those who pursue righteousness. 10 He who abandons the right path will be harshly disciplined; and those who hate correction will die. 11 Even hell holds no secrets from God; how much more does he know the human heart? 12 A mocker hates those that correct him;

they will avoid the company of the wise. 13 A cheerful heart brings a smile to your face; a broken heart crushes the spirit. 14 A wise person is thirsty for truth; but the mouth of the fool feeds on foolishness. 15 A miserable heart means a troubled life; but for the happy heart, life is a continual feast.

> *(15:14) What we put into our mind is as important as what we put into our body. The people we talk to, the music we listen to, the books we read, and the kind of movies we watch are all part of our mental nourishment. What we feed into our mind influences our overall health and well-being. A mark of wisdom is the desire to discover knowledge.*

> *(15:15) Our attitudes dictate our whole personality. We don't always have control of what happens to us, but it's up to us to choose the attitude toward each situation. Filling our mind with thoughts that are pure is the secret to a happy heart. Check your attitudes and examine what you allow to enter your mind and what you choose to dwell on and make the necessary changes.*

15:16-21 Better to have little with fear of the Lord, then to have great treasure with many troubles. 17 Eating crackers and butter with someone you love is better than having a steak dinner with someone you hate. 18 A hot-head starts trouble; but the one who is slow to anger keeps the peace. 19 The lazy person has a life of troubles; but the path of the upright is as smooth as a freeway. 20 Wise children bring joy to their father; foolish children despise their mothers. 21 Foolishness brings joy to those without sense; but those with understanding stay on the right path.

> *(18-19) The hot-head and the lazy person bring unnecessary troubles into their lives that the upright person does not have to face. The road of the upright isn't always an easy path, but in comparison, the foolish will face many more troubles in life, while the upright person's road is level because it is built on a solid foundation of love for God.*

15:22-28 Without advice, plans go wrong; but having many counselors brings success. 23 A man has joy by the answer of his mouth; how good it is to say the right thing at the right time. 24 For the wise, the way of life leads to life above; that he may turn away from hell below. 25 God destroys the house of the arrogant; and he stands with those who have no standing. 26 The thoughts of the wicked are despised by the Lord; but he delights in words that are pure. 27 He who is greedy for gain will bring trouble to his own house; but those who hate bribes will live. 28 God-loyal people think before speaking; but the mouth of the wicked spouts evil words.

(15:22) When you try to make important decisions on your own, it's highly more likely that the plans will fail. On the other hand, when you seek out the advice of those who know you well and that have experiences, your plans will be stronger and more likely to succeed. Be open to new ideas and willing to weigh suggestions carefully.

(15:28) The God-loyal choose their answers carefully. The wicked don't think before speaking because they don't care about the effects of their words. We all have something to say, but it's important to think about it first. Do you pour out your thoughts without any concern of their impact, or do you carefully plan your words?

15:29-33 The Lord keeps his distance from the wicked; but he attends to the prayers of the righteous. 30 A twinkle in the eye means joy in the heart; and good news makes for good health. 31 Listen to constructive criticism and you will live well among the wise. 32 He who rejects instruction only hurts himself; but he who listens to correction gains understanding. 33 Fear of the Lord is a school in wise living— first you learn humility, then you experience glory.

(15:31-32) By rejecting constructive criticism is a sign of being foolish, not wise. The ones that offer us constructive criticism are usually those that care about us the most. They may see things in us that we can't see in ourselves. When someone who cares about you points out a fault, don't take it as they are attacking you, take it as an act of love.

What lessons did you learn from this chapter?

_____

_____

_____

_____

_____

_____

_____

Chapter 16
EVERYTHING WITH A PLACE AND A PURPOSE

16:1-5 The preparations of the heart belong to man; but the right answer from the tongue is from the Lord. 2 The ways of a man may be pure in his own eyes; but the Lord examines the motives. 3 Put the Lord in charge of your work, and then your plans will succeed. 4 The Lord made everything for a purpose; even the wicked for the day of doom. 5 Everyone proud in heart is despised by the Lord; rest assured, none will go unpunished.

(16:1) This verse means that the outcome of our plans are in God's hands. We should partner between our efforts and God's control. We should plan and seek the advice of others, but the results are up to him. Ask for guidance as you plan, then act on your plan as you trust in him.

(16:2) People can rationalize anything, if they have no judgment of what's right or wrong. We are always trying to prove we are right. Before putting a plan into action, ask yourself: 1).Is my attitude pleasing to God? 2). Is this plan in harmony with God's truth?

(16:3) Commit your work to the Lord, but some commit it superficially. They claim the project is being done for the Lord, but truthfully, they are doing it for themselves. We must maintain a balance, trusting God as if everything depended on him, then working as if everything depended on us. Is there a specific project you are involved in right now? Have you committed it to God?

(16:4) Evil is a temporary condition in the universe, and one day, God will destroy it.

16:6-10 Guilt is banished through love and truth; and evil is avoided by fear of the Lord. 7 When a man's ways are pleasing to the Lord, he makes even his enemies live at peace with him. 8 It is better to be poor and righteous, than to be dishonest and rich. 9 A man makes his plans; but the Lord directs his steps. 10 A good leader speaks with wisdom; and he never judges unfairly.

(16;7) Put your energy into pleasing God, and our efforts to be peacemakers will make us more attractive to others around us, even our enemies. But, if not, we are still pleasing God, the only one who really matters.

16:11-17 The Lord cares about honesty in the workplace; your business is his business. 12 A good leader despises wrongdoing; sound leadership is established through righteousness. 13 A good leader prepares honest speech; and they love those who tell them the truth. 14 The anger of a leader is a deadly threat; and the wise do what they can to calm and pacify. 15 Good tempered leaders energize lives; they're like spring rain and sunshine. 16 How much better to get wisdom than gold; and to get understanding rather than silver. 17 The highway of the upright leads away from evil; he who keeps this way, preserves his soul.

(16:11) God demands honesty in every business transaction. Sometimes we feel pressured to be dishonest in order to advance or gain more profits, but there is no justification in a dishonest business practice. God demands honesty and fairness in all that we do, even in business. Ask him for the strength and courage to always be fair and honest.

(16:16) No amount of money can ever surpass the worth of wisdom. Most people have the disillusion that money is the answer to their problems and if they do gain it, they wonder why it hasn't filled them with joy and peace. Its because in their pursuit to gain worth, they never gained wisdom, the most valuable possession you can acquire.

16:18-25 Pride goes before destruction; and an arrogant spirit before a fall. 19 It is better to live humbly among the poor, than to live it up with the proud. 20 Listen to instruction and you will prosper; things work out when you trust in the Lord. 21 A wise man is known for his understanding: and if graciously presented, his instruction is appreciated. 22 Understanding is a spring of life to he who possesses it; but fools waste correction and continue their folly. 23 A man of wisdom makes a lot of sense; his words are persuasive. 24 Pleasant words are like honey; sweet to the soul and health to the body. 25 There is a path that looks harmless to a man; but look again, it leads straight to hell.

(16:20) Be open to wise instruction and trust God for the outcome. He is not in the business to lead you astray. No matter how bleak it may look now, keep the trust in him and he will come through.

(16:22) God's wisdom is a life-giving fountain that can make a person healthy, happy and alive forever. He washes away the deadly effects of sin when we live by his Word. The life-giving fountain is real. You can be enlightened by God's wisdom or you can be dragged down by the burdens of your foolishness.

16:26-33 Appetite is an incentive to work; hunger drives you to work harder. 27 An ungodly man digs up evil; from his lips come words that hurt and burn. 28 Troublemakers start fights; and gossip separates the best of friends. 29 A violent man deceives his neighbors; leading them down a path that is not good. 30 With a wink of an eye, they plot evil; without saying a word, they bring on trouble. 31 Gray hair is a crown of distinction, the award for a God-loyal life. 32 It is better to be patient than powerful; and self-control is better than conquering a city. 33 Make your motions and cast your votes; but the Lord has the final say.

(16:31) In Biblical times it was believed that gray hair was a sign of God's blessing. Young people may find glory in their youth and strength, elders can rejoice in their years of experience and practical wisdom. Gray hair is a crown of splendor. Whenever you deal with the elderly, always treat them with respect.

(16:32) Self-control is superior to the victory. The person who loses control of their temper may forfeit what they want the most. Success in business, school or home life could be ruined by not controlling your temper.

Frank LaRosa

What lessons did you learn from this chapter?

_____

_____

_____

_____

_____

_____

_____

Chapter 17
PEACE OVER CONFLICT

17:1-5 A meal of bread and water eaten in peace, is better than a great banquet with conflict. 2 A wise servant will rule over a master's disgraceful son; and will share the inheritance among the brothers. 3 The purity of silver and gold are tested with fire; but the Lord tests the heart. 4 An evildoer listens to wicked talk; liars listen to destructive words. 5 The one who mocks the poor, insults his maker; and one who rejoices over another's misfortune, will not go unpunished.

> *(17:3) It often takes the heat of trials for us to be purified. Through trials, God can show us what's in us and clears out anything that's in the way of completely trusting him. When tough times come your way, just remember that God wants to use them to strengthen your faith and purify your heart.*

> *(17:5) We should never get joy from seeing the misfortunes of others. We have never walked in their shoes to judge them. God loves them too, as he loves you. No one is immune to misfortune, and your life too could suddenly change. That just may be the punishment talked about for rejoicing another's misfortune. When you catch yourself putting down others, stop and think about who created them.*

17:6-10 Grandchildren are the crown of the elderly; and parents are the pride of their children. 7 Eloquent speech is not appropriate coming from a fool's lips; how much worse are lies from our leaders? 8 A bribe seems like a magic stone to those who give it; wherever he turns, he succeeds. 9 Whoever overlooks an offense preserves love; but whoever gossips about it separates friends. 10 A single rebuke is more effective for a wise man, than a hundred lashes on the back of a fool.

(17:7) In our present times, it's nearly a daily occurrence that our leaders are not always speaking the truth and are misleading us with their false words. Those that we should trust the most for our freedom and safety are the ones lying to us. In these days, there's a better chance to hear a fool speak with sense, than to get honesty from our leaders.

(17:8) Bribery is not being condoned here. Some people may use bribes to get what they want, but the Bible clearly condemns it.

(17:9) We should be willing to overlook the faults of others. Covering offenses is necessary in any relationship. Especially in an argument, it is tempting to bring up all the mistakes the other person has ever made. But love keeps its mouth shut. You should never bring anything into the argument that is not related to the topic being discussed. In order to grow to be more like Christ, we need to acquire the ability to forget the confessed sins of the past.

17:11-20 Evil men seek rebellion; but trouble will eventually find them. 12 Better for a man to meet a bear robbed of her cubs, than to confront a fool caught in his folly. 13 If anyone repays good with evil; evil will never leave their house. 14 The start of a quarrel is like a leak in a dam; stop it before it burst. 15 Acquitting the guilty and condemning the innocent; both are detestable to the Lord. 16 Why does a fool have money in his hand; he has no intention of buying wisdom. 17 A friend is loyal through all kinds of weather; and a brother is born to help in time of need. 18 It is poor judgment to co-sign a friend's note; to become responsible for the debt of others. 19 Anyone who loves to quarrel loves conflict; one who builds a high threshold invites injury. 20 He who has a deceitful heart finds no good; and he who has an immoral tongue falls into evil.

(17:17) What kind of friend are you? Too many people are fair-weather friends. They are around as long as the relationship is helping them and leave when it's not benefitting them. A loyal friend will be there for you, even in your worst of times. Think of your friends. Are you loyal to them? Could they count on your friendship through all kinds of weather? Be the kind of true friend the Bible encourages.

17:21-28 It is painful to be the parent of a fool; for it brings no joy to the father. 22 A joyful heart is good medicine; but a broken spirit dries up a person's strength. 23 The wicked man take bribes under the table; to corrupt the course of justice. 24 Those with understanding keep their sights on wisdom; but the eyes of a fool roam to the ends of the earth. 25 A foolish son is grief to his father; and bitterness to his mother. 26 It is wrong to fine the godly for good behavior, or to punish the upright for being honest. 27 The wise person uses few words; an even-tempered person has understanding. 28 Even fools who keep silent are thought to be wise; as long as they keep their mouths shut, they seem intelligent.

(17:24) This proverb points out the folly of chasing a fantasy. It is much better to align your goals with God's and be the kind of person he wants you to be. Think about your dreams and goals. Do they cover the really important areas of your life? Wisdom, honesty, patience and love should be the goals you seek. For they will determine your eternal future.

(17:27-28) Some benefits of remaining quiet: 1) It is the best policy if you have nothing worthwhile to say; 2) It keeps peace if what you want to say will anger someone else; 3) It allows you to listen and learn. Don't be quick or persistent to do all the talking, you could miss something important that the other person has to say.

What lessons did you learn from this chapter?

_____

_____

_____

_____

_____

_____

_____

Chapter 18
WORDS KILL, WORDS GIVE LIFE

18:1-8 The one who isolates himself seeks his own selfish desires; he rebels against all wise judgment. 2 A fool has no delight in understanding; they only want to express their own opinions. 3 When a wicked man comes, shame is soon to follow; along with dishonor and disgrace. 4 A person's words can be like life-given water; words of true wisdom are as refreshing as a flowing brook. 5 It is not right to go easy on the guilty; nor come down hard on the innocent. 6 A fool's lips lead to conflict; and his mouth provokes a beating. 7 A fool's mouth is his destruction; their lips get them into trouble. 8 A gossip's words are like tasty food; that goes down to one's innermost being.

> *(18:8) It is hard not to listen to gossip, just as hard as turning down a piece of chocolate cake. Taking just one piece of either one creates a taste for more. Just like if you were on a diet, you'd resist the piece of cake. Same with gossip, avoid listening to it or you may decide to have a second and third piece.*

18:9-17 Laziness and sloppy work are as bad as vandalism. 10 The Lord's name is a place of protection; the righteous run to it and are safe. 11 The rich think their wealth protects them; they imagine themselves safe behind it. 12 Pride goes before the downfall; but before honor comes humility. 13 Those who answer before listening are foolish and will be shamed. 14 The spirit of a man will uphold him in sickness; but who can bear a broken spirit? 15 The heart of the wise is always learning; their ears always listening for fresh insights. 16 A man's gift opens doors for him; it can put him in front of important people. 17 The first to plead his case seems right; until another comes and cross-examines him.

(18:11) Money cannot provide safety. It is not imperishable. Thieves can steal it, inflation can rob its value, or the government could cease to back it. Wealth is uncertain, while God's faithfulness is always.

(18:13, 15, 17) Never judge before getting the facts is what these three passages are saying. Listen to the facts first, be open-minded and make sure to hear both sides of the story before making any judgment.

18:18-24 You may have to draw straws to conclude an argument; it can also settle disputes between mighty opponents. 19 An offended brother is harder to win than capturing a strong city; and arguments separate friends like a gate locked with iron bars. 20 Words satisfy the mind as much as food satisfies the stomach; good words are as gratifying as a good harvest. 21 Words can kill or words can give life; they can either be poison or fruit. 22 Find a good wife and you will find a good life; and obtain the favor of the Lord. 23 The poor man pleads; the rich man answers with insults. 24 Friends come and friends go; but a real friend sticks closer than a brother.

(18:18) Ever been in a "deadlock" situation, where neither party was budging? This passage is referring to coming to a truce (drawing straws), where no one wins or admits defeat. Doing this is preserving the peace.

(18:22) God created marriage for our enjoyment and he pronounced it good. Don't be in a hurry to be married, take time to know the person well and your life together will be good and you will have God's blessing.

(18:23) It is wrong for the rich to treat the less fortunate with arrogance and contempt. They are our neighbors, just like all people are and God himself tells us to, love our neighbors as we love ourselves. God will judge such actions severely.

What lessons did you learn from this chapter?

_____

_____

_____

_____

_____

_____

_____

Chapter 19
IF YOU QUIT LISTENING

19:1-8 It is better to be poor and honest than rich and dishonest. 2 Enthusiastic devotion without knowledge is not good; a person who moves too quickly may fall into sin. 3 People ruin their lives by their own foolishness; then blame God for it. 4 Wealth attracts many friends; but poor people are avoided like a plague. 5 A false witness will not go unpunished; nor will a liar get away with their lies. 6 People flock around a generous person; everyone is a friend to the person who gives gifts freely. 7 When you're down on your luck, even family avoids you and friends don't want to be bothered. If they see you coming, they look the other way. 8 The one who acquires wisdom loves his own soul; he who keeps understanding finds success.

> *(19:1) Better to have nothing and be one people can trust, than to have a lot and not be trusted. Many people are afraid of not getting everything they want and they will give up integrity to increase their wealth. They may cheat someone, steal from employers or from stores or withhold giving any tithes, thinking only of their own gain. Are your priorities in order? Do you sacrifice integrity to increase your wealth?*

> *(19:2) Don't be in a rush. Many people are in too much of a hurry and don't evaluate before choosing and they suffer the consequences by plunging into the unknown. Be sure you know where you want to go before taking the first step, and ask God for his direction.*

> *(19:8) This proverb isn't condoning one's selfish interest, it's encouraging those who care about themselves to seek wisdom.*

19:9-16 The person who tells lies will get caught; and the person who spreads rumors will be ruined. 10 It isn't right for a fool to live the life of luxury; nor for a worker to give orders to his boss. 11 Those with good sense restrain their anger; their splendor comes from overlooking transgressions. 12 A king's anger is like a lion's roar; but his favor is as refreshing as the dew on the morning grass. 13 A foolish child is misery to a father; a nagging wife is as annoying as a constant dripping from a faucet. 14 Houses and land are an inheritance from parents; but an understanding wife comes straight from the Lord. 15 The lazy person sleeps soundly; and soon goes hungry. 16 Those who keep the commandments keep their life; careless living leads to death.

(19:9) Lying brings on more lying. People soon find themselves having to tell more lies to cover the original lie. It can keep snow-balling and forgetting what was said, leading to eventual exposure. When you tell the truth you never have to try and remember what was said. You will always remember the truth.

(19-16) To obey what God is teaching us, through his word, is self-preserving. In disobeying, we are destroying ourselves.

19:17-24 When you help the poor, you are lending to the Lord; and the Lord pays back those loans in full. 18 Discipline your children while you still have the chance; being too lenient will ruin their lives. 19 Let the short-tempered person pay their own penalty; for if you rescue them, you will have to do it again. 20 Take good counsel and accept correction, and be wise for the rest of your life. 21 Man can make many plans; but the Lord's purpose will prove superior. 22 Kindness is what is desired in a man; and being poor is better than being dishonest. 23 Fear of the Lord leads to life; he who has it will have security and protection from harm. 24 A lazy man reaches for food, but won't even bring it to his mouth.

(19:17) As our Creator, God values all of us equally, whether we are rich or poor. When we help the poor, God accepts our help as if we had offered it directly to him and he honors us for it.

(19:18) Some parents give their children anything they want, just to keep them quiet or out of their hair. But as this verse warns, it only will hurt them in the long run. Sometimes it can be painful

to discipline, but the results will prove to be well worth it, for both
your children and for you.

(19:23) Fear of the Lord means you respect the Lord. Respect for the
Lord doesn't mean we won't face troubles in this life, evil things do
happen. What this verse is saying is, if we live with healthy habits,
we can save ourselves from some unnecessary troubles when we seek
God's intervention in all areas of our lives.

19:25-29 Punish a mocker and the simpleminded will learn a lesson;
correct the wise and they will be all the wiser. 26 A child who mistreats
his father and chases away his mother, is a child that causes shame
and embarrassment. 27 Stop listening to instruction, my son, and you
turn your back on knowledge. 28 A corrupt witness mocks justice; and
a wicked mouth swallows evil. 29 Punishment awaits the mockers; and
the backs of fools will be beaten.

(19:25) There is a vast difference between the person who refuses
to accept correction and the person who learns from criticism. How
we respond will determine whether or not we grow in wisdom. Listen
carefully the next time someone criticizes or corrects you, there just
might be a lesson to be learned.

What lessons did you learn from this chapter?

_____

_____

_____

_____

_____

_____

_____

Chapter 20
CHALICE OF KNOWLEDGE

20:1-8 Wine produces mockers, liquor causes brawls; a staggering drunk cannot be wise. 2 A quick-tempered leader is like a lion's roar; anyone who angers him endangers himself. 3 It's a mark of good character to avoid quarrels; but fools love to pick fights. 4 A farmer too lazy to plow in the spring, has nothing to harvest in the fall. 5 Good advice lies deep within a man's heart; but a man of understanding can draw it out. 6 Many people claim to be loyal; but where on earth can you find a trustworthy man? 7 God-loyal people walk with integrity; and their children are blessed after them. 8 When a good leader judges, he weighs all the evidence; he recognizes the evil from the good.

(20:3) The foolish find it difficult to avoid conflict, but a person confident in their strength doesn't need to prove anything. Men & women of good character avoid conflict. What kind of person are you?

(20:4) God wants us to plan for future needs and prepare for them. When we cause our own problems through lack of planning, we can't expect him to come to our rescue. God does provide for us, but he also wants us to be responsible.

20:9-16 Who can say, "I have cleansed my heart; I am pure from my sin"? 10 Switching a price tag or padding an expense account, are two examples of things God despises. 11 Even a child is known by the way he acts; whether his conduct is pure and right. 12 Ears that hear and eyes that see; both are gifts from God. 13 Love sleep and you will end in poverty; open your eyes and get up and there will be plenty to eat. 14 The buyer cries, "It's worthless"; then brags about getting a bargain. 15 The lips that speak knowledge are more precious than gold and rubies. 16 Get collateral on a loan made for a stranger; collect a deposit if someone guarantees the debt of a foreigner.

> *(20:9) No one has the power within themselves to remove their own sin. Only God can provide forgiveness by his mercy when we ask for it. We all need ongoing cleansing. Make confession and repentance a part of your daily talks with God.*

> *(20:16) In the Hebrew text, it is written: "the debt of an adulterous woman".*

20:17-24 Food gained by fraud may taste sweet; but it soon turns to gravel in your mouth. 18 Plans succeed through good counsel; don't wage war without the advice of others. 19 Gossips can't keep secrets; never confide in someone who talks too much. 20 If you curse your father or mother; your lamp of life will be extinguished. 21 An inheritance gained early in life, is not a blessing in the end. 22 Don't ever say, "I will get even with you"; wait for the Lord, he will settle the score. 23 The Lord despises cheating in the marketplace; dishonest scales outrage him. 24 A man's steps are directed by the Lord; otherwise, how would we understand the road we're traveling?

> *(20:23) Dishonest scales refers to the loaded scales a merchant may use to cheat customers. Dishonesty is a difficult sin to avoid. Never take dishonesty lightly, it affects the very core of a person. Even a small portion of dishonesty can kill your spiritual life. Tell God now if there's any dishonesty in your life.*

> *(20:24) This proverb tells us not to worry if we don't understand the events happening around us. Sometimes it takes years before we can look back and see how God was working. We should trust that God has it under his control, even if his timing is not clear to us.*

20:25-30 It is dangerous to make a rash promise to God; then later to take back your vow. 26 A wise leader finds the wicked; then drives the crushing wheel over them. 27 The human spirit is the searchlight of the Lord; it examines us inside and out, exposing every hidden motive. 28 Love and truth form a good leader; sound leadership is founded on loving integrity. 29 The glory of the young is their strength; and the magnificence of the old is their gray hair. 30 Physical blows cleanse away evil; and such discipline purifies the heart.

(20:25) This passage points out the danger of making a rash promise and later reconsidering it. Jesus says it is better not to make any promises to God because he knows they are difficult to keep.(Matthew 5:33-37) Rash promises are better not made, then to make them and later not keep them. God takes vows seriously.

What lessons did you learn from this chapter?

_____

_____

_____

_____

_____

_____

_____

Chapter 21
God Examines Our Motives

21:1-10 Good leadership is a channel of water controlled by the Lord; he directs it wherever he chooses. 2 In his own eyes, a man may think he is doing right; but the Lord examines the heart. 3 Doing what is just and right is more pleasing to the Lord than when we give sacrifices. 4 Arrogance and pride and evil actions are all sin. 5 Careful planning and hard work lead to prosperity; hasty shortcuts lead to poverty. 6 Wealth created by lying will vanish; and you will be caught in a deadly trap. 7 The violence of the wicked will destroy them; because they refuse to do what is right. 8 The guilty walk a crooked path; the pure of heart travel a straight road. 9 Better to live alone in a run-down shack, than to live in a beautiful home with a nagging spouse. 10 Evil people love to make trouble; they have no consideration for their friends and neighbors.

> *(21:3) If our personal or business dealings are not on the up and up, no amount of generosity or sacrifice will make up for it. Sacrifices won't bribe God into overlooking our character faults.*

> *(21:5) It is a great accomplishment when we faithfully complete our work. Being a diligent worker is the result of strong character. Don't take shortcuts that may result in inefficiency. Work hard as if working directly for God.*

21:11-17 A simpleton only learns by seeing mockers punished; but the wise learn by listening. 12 The Righteous One knows what's going on in the house of the wicked; he will bring the wicked to ruin. 13 Shut your ears to the cries of the poor and you will not be heard in your time of need. 14 A quietly given gift soothes an irritable person;

a heartfelt present cools a hot temper. 15 The godly celebrate when justice is served; but it's terror to those who practice evil. 16 The man who strays from the way of wisdom will end up in the company of the dead. 17 He who loves pleasure will be poor; pursue pleasures and never be rich.

(21:11-12) Listen to the advice of others who have made the mistakes already and take heed of their instruction. It can save you from plunging ahead and learning the hard way.

(21:13) So many people turn their backs on the poor. Some even think they chose to be poor and aren't worthy of help. They, too, are God's children and we should work to meet their needs. God gives to us so we can give. Although you may not be in need today, someday you may be. Would you want people to turn their backs on you?

21:18-26 What an evil person plots against the good, will come back to him in the end. 19 Better to live alone in the desert than with a quarrelsome, complaining spouse. 20 The wise have wealth and luxury; but fools spend whatever they get. 21 Whoever pursues what is right and kind will find life, godliness, and honor. 22 The wise conquer the city of the strong; and tear down their secure forts. 23 Hold your tongue and keep yourself out of trouble. 24 A mocker is proud and snobbish; they act with boundless arrogance. 25 The desires of a lazy man will be his ruin; because he won't get up and go to work. 26 He is always greedy for more; while the godly love to give.

(21:18) You've heard the saying, "What goes around, comes around"? This could be the passage that saying came from. God sees it all, and if you plot against the good, you will suffer the consequences. It may not happen in this life, and you may think you got away with it, but don't fool yourself, God didn't forget and you will be judged for it.

(21:20) This passage is talking about saving for the future. People's desires to keep up appearances and to accumulate more drives them to spend all they have. They may even stretch their credit to the limit. A wise person puts money aside for those rainy days. God approves of restraint and looking ahead. Is your spending God-pleasing or is it self-pleasing?

21:27-31 The Lord detests the sacrifice of the wicked; especially when it is brought with ulterior motives. 28 A lying witness will be cut off; but a truthful witness will be allowed to speak. 29 A wicked man puts on a bold front; but the righteous man considers his way. 30 No human wisdom, no understanding, nor counsel, can outsmart the Lord. 31 The horse is prepared for the day of battle; but the victory comes from the Lord.

> *(21:27) The kind of sacrifice described in this passage is no more than a bribe. People may go to church, tithe or volunteer, not because of their devotion to God, but because they hope they will be blessed in return. God has made it clear that he desires love and obedience over religious ritual. God wants our hearts, not our sacrifices of time, energy, and money alone. He wants our complete love and devotion.*

> *(21:31) This passage refers to preparing for battle. Without God, all our preparations for any task are useless. Even with his help we still need to do our part. He controls the outcome, but we cannot forget our responsibilities. For example, God may want you to write a book, but it's up to you to learn to write. God's purposes will be accomplished and he will be able to use you for his purpose, if you have done your part by being well prepared.*

What lessons did you learn from this chapter?

_____

_____

_____

_____

_____

_____

_____

Chapter 22
DISCIPLINE

22:1-5 A good reputation is better than striking it rich; a gracious spirit is better than money in the bank. 2 The rich and the poor have this in common; God made them both. 3 A sensible man sees the danger ahead and takes cover; a simpleton goes on blindly and suffers the consequences. 4 The payoff for meekness and fear of the Lord is riches and honor and a satisfying life. 5 The deceitful travel a dangerous road; whoever values their soul will stay away.

(22:3) Have a plan and don't rush into anything. When we are hasty, we lose sight of any danger signs. Plan ahead and take precautions, it may save you a lot of unnecessary troubles.

(22:4) This is a general observation. The Book of Proverbs describes life the way it should be. In a perfect world wise behavior would always lead to these benefits. Even in our troubled world, living wisely can result in obvious blessings, but not always. That is why we must live by believing and not by seeing.

22:6-11 Point your children in the right direction; and when they are old they won't be lost. 7 The poor are ruled over by the rich: and the borrower is at the mercy of the lender. 8 Sow seeds of injustice and you will reap disaster; and your reign of terror will end. 9 Blessed are the generous; for they give bread to the poor. 10 Drive out a mocker and conflict goes too; then fighting and quarrels will end. 11 God loves a pure heart and gracious speech; good leaders also delight in their friendship.

(22:6) In the process of pointing your children in the right direction, we must take into concern the differing paths of each child. It's natural

to want to bring up all our children alike, but each has different strengths that God has given them. Encourage them to develop their individual capabilities as you guide them in the right direction.

(22:7) This doesn't mean we should never borrow, but it warns us to examine our ability to repay it. If you borrow, you must realize that you are at the mercy of the individual or institution that made it, until the loan is repaid in full.

22-12-16 The Lord's eyes keep watch over knowledge; but he will defeat the plans of the faithless. 13 The lazy man says, "There's a lion in the street!, If I go outside, I could be killed!" 14 The mouth of an immoral woman is a deep pit; those who are despised by the Lord will fall into it. 15 Young people are filled with foolishness; discipline drives it away. 16 Oppressing the poor to get ahead and giving to the rich; both lead to poverty.

(22:12) "Knowledge" is referring to those who live right and speak the truth. It takes hard work to live God's way, but he protects and rewards those who make the commitment to follow him. It may seem that the faithless have an easier time, but in the long run their plans fail and their lives end up empty. Resist God and you will never have lasting success.

(22:13) This excuse may sound silly, but that's how our excuses may sound to others. Don't make excuses for laziness, take responsibility and go to work.

(22:15) Kids often do foolish and sometimes dangerous things. Wisdom and common sense are not learned by a parent's good example alone. God trains and corrects us to make us better, and as a parent, we must discipline our children and teach them the difference between right and wrong.

Sayings of the Wise
22:17-29 Listen carefully to my words of wisdom; take to heart what I can teach you. 18 For it is good to keep these saying deep within yourself; always ready on your lips. 19 So you will trust in the Lord, I'm laying it all out right now, just for you. 20 I have written thirty saying for you; all filled with advice and knowledge. 21 Believe me, these are truths that work; and you can bring back an accurate report to those who sent you.

22 Don't walk on the poor just because they are poor, or use your position to crush the weak. 23The Lord will come to their defense; he will injure anyone who injures them. 24 Don't hang out with angry, short-tempered people, 25 or you will learn to be like them and endanger your soul. 26 Do not co-sign another person's note or guarantee someone's loan. 27 If you can't pay it, you'll be left with nothing but the shirt on your back. 28 Do not steal your neighbor's property by moving the boundary lines set up by your ancestors. 29 Do you see a man truly competent in his work? He will serve leaders, not ordinary people.

(22:22-23) This proverb is a message of hope to those who live and work under unjust leaders. It is also a warning to forceful rulers. God may intervene directly or indirectly, to throw out these kinds of leaders. By indirectly, he may use other leaders to overthrow them or their own people to rebel against them. Leadership through kindness is more effective and lasts longer than leadership by force.

(22:24-25) People tend to become like those they spend a lot of time with. Both good and negative characteristics can rub off. The Bible tells us to be cautious of who we hang out with. Choose people with qualities you would like to develop in your own life.

(22:28) Boundaries in Israel were sacred because God owned the land and he apportioned the property to the tribes. To extend one's property illegally by moving a neighbor's boundary marker was a violation of covenant and oath. Of course, disputes could arise when both sides claim their ancestors established a boundary.

(22:29)Solomon was a sitting king when he wrote this and he was, no-doubt, surrounded by a skilled and talented staff. Those in authority are always looking for the 'best of the best' to be on their staffs. Here Solomon says that those who are exceptionally good at what they do will find themselves working for kings, not for the average or unknown leader. If you work diligently and skillfully, expeditious, industriously pursuing excellence, cheerfully attending to your tasks, and not growing weary of your work, you will be noticed and promoted.

What lessons did you learn from this chapter?

_____

_____

_____

_____

_____

_____

_____

Chapter 23
RESTRAIN YOURSELF

23:1-5 When you dine with an influential person, pay attention to what is before you. 2 If you are a big eater, restrain yourself from eating too much, 3 and don't desire all the delicacies. For deception may be involved. 4 Don't wear yourself out trying to get rich. 5 Riches can disappear as if they had the wings of a bird.

> *(23:1-3) The point here is to be cautious when dining with a person of importance because they may be offering all this food and delicacies trying to bribe you. No good will come from the meal.*

> *(23:4-5) Like the people who have won millions of dollars and lost everything, even the average person can spend an inheritance, or a paycheck, in the blink of an eye and have nothing to show for it. Don't spend your time chasing earthly treasures. The only treasures that will never be lost are the treasures we store up in Heaven.*

23:6-11 Don't eat with people who are stingy; and don't desire their choice food. 7 He'll be as stingy with you as he is with himself. "Eat! Drink!", he says to you, but he won't mean a word of it. 8 You will vomit up the food they serve, and have to take back your words of appreciation. 9 Don't bother talking sense to fools; they will only despise your words of wisdom. 10 Don't move the ancient property lines and cheat the orphans of what's theirs. 11 For they have a mighty Redeemer and he himself will take their case against you.

> *(23:6-8) This is a warning not to be envious of those who have gained riches by being stingy and cheap, and not to gain their*

*favor by making over them. Their friendship is phony and will
only use you for their own gain.*

*(23:10) This proverb is saying to not take advantage of people,
especially the less fortunate that may not have the resources
or the knowhow to defend themselves. Moving a property line
to give yourself more land is stealing what isn't yours. A sin
God will judge severely.*

23:12-18 Be open to instruction; and listen to the words of knowledge. 13 Don't fail to correct your children; if you spank them they won't die. 14 Physical discipline, in fact, may save them from hell. 15 My child, if you become wise, how happy I will be. 16 Yes, my heart will rejoice when you speak what is right and true. 17 Don't be envious of sinners; be always fearful of the Lord. 18 For surely there is a hereafter, and your hope will not be disappointed.

*(23:13-14) Some parents fear to discipline their children. They
fear it may harm their relationship, or that their children might
resent them. Correction won't kill children and it just may prevent
them from doing foolish things that will.*

*(23:17-18) Don't be envious of those who get ahead, paying no
attention to God's law. For a while they may seem to prosper, but
their future will suffer. God promises a hope and a glorious future
to those who trust in and follow him. Don't let it phase you of what
the unfaithful may have now. You have one thing they don't have, the
promise from God of a wonderful, eternal future.*

23:19-30 Listen to me, my child, and be wise; keep your heart of the right path. 20 Don't get mixed up with those who drink too much; or with those who gorge themselves with food. 21 For drunks and gluttons will become poor; they will sleep too much and find themselves dressed in rags. 22 Listen to your father who raised you; and don't neglect your mother when she is old. 23 Buy the truth and never sell it; buy wisdom, buy discipline, buy knowledge. 24 Parents rejoice when their child turns out well; a wise child is their delight. 25 So make your father happy; and make your mother proud. 26 My child, give me your full attention; and do as I have shown you. 27 A prostitute is like a dark pit; and a seductive woman can get you into deep trouble. 28 She's worse than a thief in the night; looking for men who will be unfaithful to their wives. 29 Who has intense misery? Who has sorrow? Who is always in conflicts? Who is always complaining? Who has bruises for no reason? Who has bloodshot eyes? 30 It is the one who spends all night in the bars, drinking and drinking.

> *(23:29-30) You've heard the saying, "I'm going to drink away my sorrows". The problem is, the comfort of alcohol is only temporary. People respond differently to alcohol. Some may get overly happy, which can annoy others, while others can become mean and violet and can cause more troubles for themselves and others. Real relief only comes from dealing with the source of the misery and sorrow and turning to God for peace.*

23:31-35 Don't judge wine by its sparkle and smooth taste. 32 Judge it by the after effects; the splitting headache, the queasy stomach. 33 You will see double and you will say crazy things. 34 You will stagger like you were walking on the deck of a ship in rough seas. 35 And you will say, "They hit me, but I wasn't hurt; they beat me, but I didn't feel anything. When I'm sober again, bring me another drink!"

> *(23:31-35) It is written as wine, but these passages refer to all alcohol. It dulls the senses, it limits clear judgment, it lowers our capacity of self-control, and it destroys one's efficiency. By misusing it or using it as an escape from life, can bring on serious consequences.*

What lessons did you learn from this chapter?

_____
_____
_____
_____
_____
_____

Chapter 24
Intelligence Over Muscle

24:1-6 Don't be envious of bad people; don't even desire to be in their company. 2 All they think about is plotting violence; and their words only stir up trouble. 3 It takes wisdom to build a house; and its foundation becomes strong through good sense. 4 By knowledge the rooms are furnished with fine furniture and beautiful draperies. 5 It is better to be wise than to be strong; intelligence over muscle any day. 6 Never go to war without wise guidance; to be victorious you will need many counselors.

> *(24:1-2) We tend to take on traits of those we hang around with. Hanging out with those who talk bad about others or always stirring up trouble, you are bound to find trouble. Don't seek their company. Instead, seek those who have quality traits that will help bring out your best qualities and character.*

> *(24:5) Anyone who has wisdom, who studies the situation and plans a strategy, has a huge advantage over a stronger, but unwise opponent. We exercise and eat well to build our strength, but many don't take on the pains to develop wisdom and knowledge, which is a vital part of our strength.*

> *(24:6) In any major decision we face, it is wise to ask for advice. It is not a sign of weakness, instead, it is foolish not to ask. Good advisers can help you evaluate your choices and help you make the best choice.*

24:7-12 Wisdom is way over the head of a fool; in a serious discussion, they have no idea what to say. 8 The one who plots to do evil will be known as a troublemaker. 9 A foolish scheme is sin; and a mocker is despised by everyone. 10 If you fall to pieces in a difficult time, your strength is not very strong. 11 Rescue those unjustly sentenced to death; don't hesitate to step in and help. 12 Don't avoid responsibility by saying, "We didn't know about it". God knows all hearts and he sees you. Doesn't he watch over our souls and knows we knew? Does he not judge all people according to what they have done?

(24:8) Plotting evil can be as wrong as doing it, because your thoughts can determine what you will do and can lead to sin. Planning evil brings sinful thoughts into our minds. Before acting on the thought, stop and ask for God's forgiveness and ask him to steer you onto a different path.

(24:10) Times of trouble can show who you really are---Your true character, and they can help you grow stronger. After questioning God, God asked Jeremiah how he expected to handle a big challenge, if a small one tired him out (Jeremiah 12:5). Don't complain about your problems, they are training you to be stronger for a more difficult situation you may face in the future.

24:13-18 Eat honey, my child, for it is good for you; and the honeycomb is sweet to your taste. 14 And realize, in the same way, wisdom is sweet to your soul. Find wisdom and your future is secure; and your hopes will never fade. 15 Don't interfere with the lives of the godly; and don't try to destroy where they live. 16 They may fall seven times, but they will get up each time. But the wicked will end up flat on their faces. 17 Do not rejoice when your enemy falls into trouble. And don't let your heart be glad when he stumbles. 18 For the Lord might see and become displeased with you, and then take pity on his predicament.

(24:17-18) To rejoice over someone's misfortune is like taking vengeance on them and putting yourself in place of God, who alone is the real judge of all the earth. Solomon's father, David, refused to rejoice over the death of his enemy, Saul. But the nation of Edom rejoiced over Israel's defeat and was punished by God for their attitude.

24:19-26 Do not worry yourself because of evildoers; and don't wish you could succeed like the wicked. 20 Those people have no future; they're headed down a dead-end street. 21 My child, fear the Lord and respect your leaders; and don't associate with persons who resist authority. 22 For you will go down with them, when their life turns upside down; and who knows how or when it might happen?

More Sayings of the Wise

23 Here are further sayings of the wise: It is wrong to show favoritism when passing judgment. 24 He who says to the wicked, "You are innocent", will be cursed by the people and condemned publicly by the nations. 25 But those who convict the guilty will have delight; and a good blessing will come upon them. 26 Receiving an honest answer is like receiving a warm hug.

(24:24) We've seen this happen in today's society. Think of the two famous murder trials in recent years, where the accused were found innocent, when the guilt was evident. The public's reaction was just as it is written in this passage. But God sees all and the due justice will eventually be served. Maybe not in this life, but when Jesus returns.

(24:26) People often think they should bend the truth to avoid hurting a friend, but one who gives an honest, straight forward answer is a "true" friend.

24:27-34 First, complete your outdoor work and plant your fields; then build your house. 28 Do not talk about your neighbors behind their backs; don't lie about them. 29 Don't say, "I'll get you back for what you did to me. I'll get even with you!" 30 One day I walked by the field of a lazy man; and then by the vineyard of a man lacking sense. 31 They were overgrown with thorns, covered with weeds and all the fences were broken down. 32 I looked and thought about it, and I learned this lesson: 33 A little extra sleep, a nap here and there, and too many days off, 34 and poverty will be your permanent houseguest!

(24:27) We should carry out our work in proper order. A farmer will miss the planting season, if he builds his house in the spring, and go a year without food. If a businessman's business is struggling to grow and he invests his money in a house, he may lose both. It is possible to work hard and still lose everything if the timing is wrong or the resources are not in place to carry it out.

(24:29) Here is a reverse version of the Golden Rule: "Do for others as you would like them to do for you (Luke 6:31). Revenge is a way of the world, but it is not God's way. Instead, pray for those who do wrong to you and then leave the justice in God's hands.

What lessons did you learn from this chapter?

_____

_____

_____

_____

_____

_____

_____

Chapter 25
FURTHER WISE SAYINGS OF SOLOMON

25:1-5 These too are proverbs of Solomon, copied by the men of King Hezekiah of Judah. 2 It is the delight of God to conceal things; but scientist delight in discovering things. 3 No one knows the height of Heaven, or the depth of the earth, or all that goes on in the hearts of good leaders. 4 Remove impurities from the silver, and the silversmith can craft a fine chalice. 5 Remove the wicked from leadership, and authority will be righteous and God-honoring.

(25:1) Hezekiah was one of the few kings in Judah that honored God. He restored the Temple, destroyed idol worship centers and earned respect from the surrounding nations.

25:6-13 Do not glorify yourself in the presence of the king; don't push for a place among the well-known. 7 It is better to wait for an invitation than to be dishonored and humiliated. Just because you see something, 8 Do not be hasty to go to court; for in the end, your neighbor might put you to shame. 9 Instead, discuss the matter with them privately; and do not tell anyone else. 10 Or word is sure to get around and no one will trust you. 11 The right word spoken at the right time is as wonderful as apples of gold, in a sterling silver setting. 12 A wise friend's valid reprimand is as treasured as jewelry made from the finest gold. 13 Reliable friends are as refreshing as snow in the heat of the summer; they are refreshing to the soul.

(25:6) Jesus made a parable of this. Luke 14:7-11, it reads: "If you are invited to a feast, don't always run to get the best seat. What if someone more respected has also been invited? Then the host may say, 'Let this person sit here'. Then you will

*be embarrassed and sent to sit wherever you can at the foot of the
table. I say, do this instead, sit at the foot of the table, then when
your host sees you he will come and say, 'We have a better place
for you. Then you will honored before all the other guests. For
the proud will be humbled, and the humble will be honored.*

25:14-20 The person who falsely brags about giving, is like clouds
and wind without any rain. 15 Patience can persuade a ruler; and
soft speech can break down rigid defenses. 16 If you're given a box of
sweets, don't eat too much, or you'll make yourself sick. 17 Do not visit
your friends too often, or they may resent you and your welcome will
wear out. 18 Spreading lies about someone is just as harmful as hitting
them with a bat, stabbing them with a sword, or shooting them with
an arrow. 19 Trusting in an unreliable person in times of trouble, is
like biting down on an abscessed tooth or walking on a broken foot.
20 Singing cheerful songs to a person, whose heart is heavy, is like
pouring salt into a wound.

*(25:14) Many who make promises to give, fail to follow
through. Some may even brag to others that they give
gifts, so others will think they are faithful when they are
not backing what they are saying. Churches, missions and
Christian groups depend on the generosity of people to
keep their ministries going. You may think that your one
gift wouldn't matter overall, but if everyone had the same
thinking, then no church or organizations would survive. If
you make a pledge, keep your word.*

*(25:17) Friends and relatives are happy to see us when they
haven't seen us in a while, but if you visit someone's house
too often, popping in unannounced at all hours, they will soon
be annoyed with you and resent your presence. Although it is
good to stay in contact with our friends and family, avoid wearing
out your welcome with your presence too often.*

*(25:18) It is vicious to lie about someone. Effects from it can be
as permanent as those of a wound. Reputations can be destroyed
and friends can be lost. The victim of the lie may have a lot of
unnecessary "proving" to do, causing them anxiety and stress
over something that was not even true. The next time you are*

tempted to pass on a bit of gossip, imagine yourself stabbing that person with a sword.

25:21-28 If your enemy is hungry, give him food to eat; if he is thirsty, give him water to drink. 22 Your generosity will surprise him and the Lord will reward you. 23 Just as a north wind brings forth rain, a mouth that gossips causes anger. 24 Better to live alone in a run-down shack than to share a beautiful home with an argumentative spouse. 25 Receiving good news from far away is like a cold drink of water to the thirsty. 26 A good person who gives in to a bad person is like throwing mud into a clean spring or a polluting a fountain. 27 Just as it is not good to stuff yourself with sweets; it is not good for people to think about all the glory they deserve. 28 A person who cannot control himself is as defenseless as a fort without walls.

(25:21) In Matthew 5:44, Jesus tells us to pray for those who hurt us. As difficult as it can be, by returning good for evil, we are acknowledging God as the balancer and trusting him to be the judge.

(25:24) We've seen this passage written twice in Prov 21, verses 9 & 19, and now again in this chapter. To live together with someone who is dramatic and argumentative can drain you of your spirit. This person will usually find fault with everyone around them, but rarely, if ever, see fault in themselves. Living with such a person is extremely difficult, and as this passage says, 'it's better to live alone', or you may never be able to be the best you can be. We should pray for these people and ask God to change their negative attitudes.

(25:27) To dwell on the glory you think you deserve, can only be harmful. It may make you bitter, discouraged or angry, and it still won't bring the honors you think should be yours. Instead of dwelling on what you feel you should have received, be satisfied knowing you did your best.

(25:28) Self-control, undoubtedly, limits us, but it is necessary. A life that is out-of-control is open to many sorts of attacks by the enemy. Think of self-control as the walls of a fort that are for defense and protection.

Frank LaRosa

What lessons did you learn from this chapter?

_____

_____

_____

_____

_____

_____

_____

_____

Chapter 26
Fools Repeat Foolishness

26:1-7 To give honor to fools is like snow falling in the summer or raining during harvest. 2 Like a swift moving sparrow or a dashing bird; an undeserved curse will not land on its intended victim. 3 Guide a racehorse with a whip, a donkey with a bridle, and a fool with a stick to the back. 4 Don't respond to a fool's foolish arguments; or you'll look just as foolish. 5 Answer a fool's argument with a foolish answer; or in his own eyes he may think himself wise. 6 To send a message by way of a fool is as foolish as cutting off your own foot or purposely drinking poison. 7 A proverb quoted by a fool is as limp as a paralyzed leg.

(25:2) "An undeserved curse will not land" means that it has no effect.

(25:4-5) These two verses may seem to contradict each other, but what is being said is that we should not try and reason with the argument of a fool. This will only make them determined to win the argument. In some situations, it's better to not even try answering, for there is no way to get through to their closed mind and you may bring yourself down to their level if you answer. A fool will abuse you and you may be tempted to retaliate with abuse in return. But there are other situations where your common sense tells you to answer in order to expose their pride and folly.

(26:7) There are some people so blind that they won't get much wisdom from reading these Proverbs. Only those that sincerely want to be wise will have the receptive attitude to learn by them. God will respond and pour out his heart to us, if we earnestly desire to learn from him.

26:8-12 Giving honor to a fool is like tying a stone to a slingshot. 9 Putting a scalpel in a drunks hand is just as dangerous as asking a fool to quote a proverb. 10 Hiring a fool or a drunk would be like shooting yourself in the foot. 11 Just as a dog returns to its vomit, so does a fool repeat his foolishness. 12 There is more hope for a fool than for a man who is wise in his own eyes.

> *(26:8) If you give a fool some privilege and responsibility, to try and make him loyal and productive, it usually doesn't work. It's like tying a stone to a slingshot, it won't go anywhere and can sling back and hurt you. A fool's new power could be just what he needed to manipulate others.*

> *(26:9) A fool may not feel the sting of a proverb because he doesn't see how it may apply to his own life. Instead of taking the proverb's point to heart, a fool will apply it to whomever he is rebelling against, saying, "they should really pay attention to this". When the fact is, they should be asking themselves, "Is there a message in it for me?"*

26:13-19 The lazy person makes up all kinds of excuses to not leave the house; "It's dangerous out there! I'm sure there's a lion in the street!", then pulls the covers back over his head. 14 Just as a door turns on its hinges; a lazy man turns over in his bed. 15 Some people are so lazy that they won't even lift a finger to feed themselves. 16 In his own eyes, the lazy man thinks he is much wiser than seven wise counselors. 17 Butting into a quarrel that is none of your business is as foolish as yanking on the ears of a mad dog. 18 It is just as damaging as a madman shooting a lethal weapon; 19 As it is to lie to a friend and say, "I was only joking".

> *(26:13) Any person not willing to work can make up useless excuses to avoid it. Laziness can be more dangerous than a lion in the street. Pray for the strength and persistence to overcome laziness. To keep your excuses from making you useless, stop making useless excuses.*

> *(26:17) Yanking a mad dog's ears is a good way to get bitten. Interfering in a quarrel is a good way to get hurt. A lot of times the quarrelers will turn on the person who butts in. It is simply best to keep out of quarrels that do not concern you. If you have to get involved, wait until they have stopped and cooled off a bit. Only then will you have a chance to help them mend their differences.*

26:20-28 When you run out of wood, the fire goes out; when the gossip ends, the conflict dies down. 21 A quarrelsome person starts fights as easily as lighter fluid starts a fire. 22 The words of a gossip are like tasty food; they are absorbed into a person's inner most body. 23 Smooth talk may hide an evil heart, just as glaze can hide the cracks in pottery. 24 A hateful person may shake your hand and greet you pleasantly; then turn and plot against you. 25 When they speak kindly to you, don't believe them for a minute, they're just waiting for the chance to deceive you. 26 While they may think they're sly in concealing their evil heart, eventually their evil will be publicly exposed. 27 Whoever sets a trap for others, will get caught in it themselves. Try rolling a boulder over someone and it will roll back and crush you. 28 A lying tongue hates its victims; and a mouth that speaks flattery causes ruin.

> *(26:20) Talking about every little irritation and piece of gossip only keeps the fires of anger fueled. Refusing to discuss them cuts the fuel line and makes the fires die out. Is there someone who continually irritates you? Choose not to complain about that person and you may see your irritation die out from the lack of fuel.*

What lessons did you learn from this chapter?

_____

_____

_____

_____

_____

_____

_____

Chapter 27
You Don't Know What Tomorrow Will Bring

27:1-10 Don't brag about what you're going to do tomorrow; for you don't know the first thing about tomorrow. 2 Do not praise yourself; let others do that for you. 3 A stone is heavy and sand is weighty; but putting up with a fool's silliness outweighs them both. 4 Fury is cruel and anger is like a violent downpour of rain; but who is able to withstand the destructiveness of jealousy? 5 A spoken reprimand is better than love that is never expressed. 6 The wounds from a loyal friend are worth it; but the kisses from an enemy are full of deceit. 7 Honey has no taste to a person with a full belly; but even bitter food is sweet to the hungry. 8 An unsettled man that is constantly wandering to and fro, is like a restless bird who wanders from its nest. 9 The heartfelt counsel of a loyal friend is as sweet as the smell of the finest perfume. 10 Don't abandon your friends or your father's friends and run to your family in a time of need. Better to have a nearby friend, than to have a family far away.

> *(27:5) Many people don't receive a reprimand well. They'll take it as criticism and that you're just pointing out their faults and not see it as a genuine concern to help them better themselves. To reprimand someone you care about is an act of expressing love for them. Love isn't always pleasant, but it's better than not expressing love at all.*

> *(27:6) A loyal friend, who has your best interests at heart, may have to give you unpleasant advice from time to time, but coming from a friend, you know it's for your own good. An enemy may whisper pleasant words to you, then send you on your way to ruin. We all have a tendency to only hear what we want to hear, even if*

*our enemy is the only one who will say it. No matter how painful
it may be, a true friend's advice is something we should treasure.*

27:11-18 My child, if you become wise, how happy I will be; then
nothing the world could throw my way will upset me. 12 The sensible
person sees the dangers ahead and takes precautions; the foolish
ignore the dangers and suffer the consequences. 13 Get collateral on
a loan made for a stranger; collect a deposit if someone guarantees
the debt of an adulterous woman. 14 If you shout a pleasant greeting
to your neighbor too early in the morning, it will sound to him more
like a curse than a blessing. 15 A nagging spouse is just as annoying as
the constant drip of a leaky faucet. 16 Trying to stop it is like trying to
hold back the wind or trying to hold something with greased hands.
17 As iron sharpens iron; a friend sharpens a friend. 18 If you tend to
your orchard, you will enjoy its fruit; and if you look after the interests
of your employer, you will be rewarded.

*(27:13) In this passage the "debt of an adulterous woman" is
referring to anyone that you don't know well or that may not
be very trusting. If you do guarantee the debt, be sure to protect
yourself by securing some sort of collateral.*

*(27:15) Quarrelsome nagging is a like a form of torture. People
nag when they think they're not getting through, but nagging
hinders communication more than it helps. When you are
tempted to partake in this destructive habit, stop and examine
what your motive is. Is it that you are more concerned about
yourself, getting your way and being right, than about the other
person you are pretending to help? If you are truly concerned
about helping other people, think of a more pleasant way to
get through to them. Words of patience and love may just be
what the doctor ordered.*

*(27:17) There is a mental sharpness that comes from being around
good people. A meeting of the minds can help people see their ideas
with new clarity, refine and shape them into ingenious insights. This
requires people who focus on the idea and that leave their own egos
out of the discussion. Two friends who bring their ideas together can
help each other become sharper.*

*(27:18) With all that's on the plate of a leader, it can be easy to over-
look faithful employees or volunteers. The very people who stand
behind you, who work hard and get the job done, deserve to share in*

your success. Be sure that in all your planning, organizing and working, you don't overlook or forget the people that are helping you the most.

27:19-23 Just like water reflects your face, your heart reveals who you really are. 20 Just as Death and Destruction are never satisfied; the desires of man are never satisfied. 21 The purity of silver and gold is tested by putting them into the fire; the purity of the human heart is tested by giving the person a little fame. 22 No matter what you do or how hard you try, you can't separate a fool from his foolishness

(27:21) A "little fame" tests a person, just like high temperatures test metal. How a person handles fame (or praise) can tell a lot about their character. People of integrity are not swayed by being praised or well-known. They are attuned to their inner convictions and they do what they should whether they are noticed for it or not.

27:23-27 Know the condition of your flock; and pay close attention to your herds. 24 For riches don't last forever; and even a crown is not guaranteed to be passed down to the next generation. 25 And then, when the crops are harvested and stored in the barn, 26 you can knit clothing from the lamb's wool and sell your goats for a good profit. 27 And you will have enough milk and food to last your family through the winter.

(27:23-27) Life is uncertain and we should be persistent in preparing for the future. We should be responsible stewards, like a farmer with land and herds. We should act with foresight, giving attention to our home, our family and our career. For God's people, thinking ahead is a duty, not an option.

What lessons did you learn from this chapter?

_____
_____
_____
_____
_____
_____

Chapter 28
IF YOU REJECT GOD'S LAW

28:1-8 The wicked are full of guilt and ready to run away, when no one's chasing them; but the righteous are relaxed and confident, bold as lions. 2 When there is moral rot within a nation, its government crumbles easily; and it will take leaders with real understanding to straighten things out. 3 A wicked man who persecutes the poor is like a hailstorm that destroys the crops. 4 If you reject God's law you are praising the wicked; but those who keep His law battle against them. 5 The evil do not understand justice; but those who seek God understand it completely. 6 It is better to be poor and honest than rich and crooked. 7 The young who follow the law are wise; but those who hang out with a trouble-making crowd bring shame to their parents. 8 A man who makes money by cheating and extortion will lose it; and eventually it will end up in the hands of someone who is kind to the poor.

> *(28:2) For a government or society to survive it needs wise, unselfish leaders, which are hard to find. Each person's selfishness can quickly affect others. A selfish employer who steals from his company destroys its productivity. A selfish spouse who has an affair usually breaks up several families. When people live for themselves with little concern of how their actions affect others, the resulting moral rot can eventually contaminate an entire nation. Examine yourself. Are you the solution or part of the problem?*

28:9-12 God doesn't hear the prayers of those who ignore his law. 10 The one who leads good people down a wrong path will fall into his own pit; but the honest will inherit what is good. 11 The rich see themselves as wise; but the poor can see right through them. 12

When a righteous man succeeds, there is great rejoicing; but when the wicked come into power, people will go into hiding.

> *(28:9) If we intend to go back to our sin, God won't listen to our prayers. However, he listens, when we forsake our sin, no matter how bad, and follow him. What closes his ears is not how profound our sin may be, but our secret intention to do it again.*

> *(28:11) The rich often think they are wonderful and take credit for all they do, and not dependent on no one. It's hollow self-esteem. Through dependency on God in their struggles, the poor man may develop a richness of spirit that no amount of money can provide. The rich can lose all their material wealth, but a poor man's character can never be taken away. Don't envy the rich, money may be all they'll ever have.*

28:13-18 The one who conceals his sins will not prosper; but whoever confesses and renounces them will find mercy. 14 Happy is the one who is tenderhearted; but one who hardens his heart is headed for serious trouble. 15 A wicked leader is as dangerous to the poor as a lion or a bear attacking them. 16 A leader who lacks understanding can sink a nation; but for one who hates corruption, the future is bright. 17 A murderer burdened with guilt will be a fugitive until death. Don't protect him. 18 The one who lives with integrity will be rescued from harm; but the one who distorts right and wrong, will be destroyed.

> *(28:13) It is human nature to hide our sins or overlook our mistakes. But it's impossible to learn from a mistake you don't acknowledge making. To learn from a mistake, you need to admit it, confess it, analyze it, and make the necessary adjustments so it doesn't happen again. Something in each of us resists admitting when we are wrong. That is why we admire people who openly and graciously admit their mistakes and faults. These people have a strong self-image and they don't always have to be right to feel good about themselves. Be willing to admit when you are wrong. The first step towards forgiveness is confession.*

> *(28:17-18) A murderer's conscience will drive him into either guilt, resulting in repentance, or to death itself because of their refusal to repent. It is no act of kindness if you try to make them feel better. The more guilt, the more likely they'll turn to God and repent. If we interfere with the natural consequences of their act, we make it easier for them to return and sin again.*

28:19-28 Work hard and have plenty of food;play around and you'll end up with an empty plate. 20 Committed and persistent work will pay off; but get-rich-quick schemes will only get you into trouble. 21 To show favoritism is never a good thing; because even for something as small as a piece of bread a man will sin. 22 A greedy man tries to get rich quick; yet, little does he know, it will only lead to poverty. 23 In the end, strong reprimand is appreciated far more than flattery. 24 Anyone who robs from his parents, then asks, "What's wrong with that?", is just as bad as the one who commits murder. 25 Greed causes fighting; trusting in God leads to prosperity. 26 He who trusts in himself is a fool; but those who walk in wisdom will be safe. 27 The one who gives to the poor will lack nothing; but one who turns his eyes away will receive many curses. 28 When the wicked take charge, people go into hiding; but when they are destroyed, the righteous multiply.

(28:26) We admire the bold, self-directed people who know what they want and fight for it. They are self-reliant and neither give nor ask advice. But this is in contrast to God's law. A person doesn't know the future or predict the consequences of their choices with certainty. And so the totally self-reliant person is doomed to fail. A truly wise person depends totally on God.

(28:27) God wants us to identify with the needed and not ignore them. If we helped others when they are facing troubles, they will do whatever they can to return the favor. The Bible promises that God will supply all our needs and he usually does this through other people. What can you do today to help God supply someone's need?

What lessons did you learn from this chapter?

_____

_____

_____

_____

_____

_____

_____

Chapter 29
REFUSING TO ACCEPT CORRECTION

29:1-8 Whoever stubbornly refuses to accept criticism will see a day when life tumbles and they break; but then it will be too late to help them. 2 When good people are in charge, everyone is glad; when a wicked man rules, everyone groans. 3 If you love wisdom, you'll bring joy to your parents;but if you hang around with prostitutes, you'll destroy their trust and waste your wealth. 4 A just leader brings stability to his nation; but one who demands contributions destroys it. 5 A flattering neighbor is up to no good; he's probably setting a trap to take advantage of you. 6 Evil people are trapped by their sin; but the righteous are singing and rejoicing. 7 The godly understand what it's like to be poor; but the wicked don't care to know. 8 Mockers can get a whole town in an uproar; but those who are wise can calm everyone down.

(29:1) Those that are self-righteous never see fault in themselves and therefore refuse to accept criticism. No one is without fault and when we ignore correction we are losing out on learning wisdom and setting ourselves up for trouble.
A part of gaining wisdom is learning from our faults and accepting correction from others who see the faults we don't see in ourselves. If correction is continually ignored, and life begins to tumble, no one may want to help you because they may feel it will be a waste of time. Then you might find yourself stuck in the bed you made for yourself from not being open to criticism. Do you take correction well?

(29:5) There's a saying, "Flattery will get you everywhere". Usually when someone is up to no good they will use flattery to smooth over the person they are planning on taking advantage of or wanting something from. In our immoral world, men will use flattery to persuade a woman into having sex. Whatever the reason for the

flattery, it will usually come from the person who wants something in return.

29:9-15 If a wise man tries working things out with a fool, he is only wasting his time; he will just get scorned and ridiculed for his trouble. 10 The wicked hate the honest; but the upright seek them out. 11 A fool vents all his anger; but a wise man holds his in check. 12 If a leader listens to liars, all his advisors will become wicked. 13 The poor and their abusers have one thing in common; the Lord gave light to the eyes of both. 14 When a leader is fair to the poor, his leadership will gain authority and respect. 15 To discipline and reprimand a child produces wisdom; but an undisciplined child is an embarrassment to his parents.

(29:9) Ever tried to get through to someone who just won't listen? They become indignant and retaliate by throwing daggers your way, cutting you down and ridiculing you, picking out every fault they can find in you and use them as their defense. In these cases it's best to let them learn the hard way. For anything you say to try and get through, will be a waste of time. Pray for them and then leave it in God's hands.

(29:15)Parents often get weary of disciplining young children. They feel like all they do is nag, scold and punish. Sometimes you feel like giving up and just letting them do what they want. And then you may wonder if you've blew any chance for a loving relationship with them. When you feel that way, just remember that a kind, firm correction helps them learn and learning makes them wise. Consistent, loving discipline will, in return, teach them to discipline themselves.

29:16-21 When the wicked take charge, sin increases; but the godly will live to witness their collapse. 17 Discipline your children, and in return, they will give you happiness and peace of mind. 18 People who do not accept divine guidance, stumble all over themselves; but whoever obeys the law is blessed. 19 A worker will not be corrected by words alone, discipline is needed. Although he understands the words, they go in one ear and out the other. 20 There is more hope for a fool than for someone who talks before they think. 21 A servant pampered from childhood will later become a rebel.

(29:18) "Divine guidance" is the words from God which the prophets received. Take God out of the equation and crime and sin run rampant. Public mortality depends on knowledge of God and also on keeping his laws. In order for nations and people to function well, we must know God's ways and keep his rules.

29:22-27 An angry man stirs up conflict; and a hot-tempered man has an abundance of sin. 23 A man's pride ends in humiliation; but the humble retain honor. 24 Assist a thief and only hurt yourself; if you report his crime you too will be punished, but if you don't you will be cursed. 25 Fearing man is a dangerous trap; but trusting in the Lord brings safety. 26 Many seek the favor of a ruler; but justice comes from God. 27 The upright despise the wicked; the wicked despise the upright.

(29:24) This passage is saying that a thief's accomplice will lie under oath, and by his perjury, will only be hurting himself.

(29:25) Fear of people can hinder everything you do. Some are even afraid to leave their homes. But, respect, reverence and trust (fear in God), is liberating. Why should we fear people who can do us no eternal harm? Trust in God and he can turn the harm intended by others into good for those who trust him.

What lessons did you learn from this chapter?

_____

_____

_____

_____

_____

_____

_____

Chapter 30
GOD? WHO NEEDS HIM?

The Sayings of Agur

30:1 The words of Agur, son of Jakeh. I am weary, O God; I am weary and worn out.

> *Little is known about Agur, except that he was a wise teacher who may have come from Lemuel's kingdom and little is known about Lemuel also, except that he was a king who received wise teachings from his mother. His name means "devoted to God". Some believe he and Agur were both from the kingdom of Massa in northern Arabia. However, the origin of these sayings is not clear*

30:2-4 Surely I am more ignorant than any human is, and I do not have the common sense of a man. 3 I have not learned human wisdom, nor do I have any knowledge of the Holy One. 4 Who has gone up to Heaven and come back down? Who holds the wind and can control it with his hands? Who has gathered up the waters of the ocean in his cloak? Who has established all the ends of the earth? What is his name and what is his Son's name? Tell me if you know!

> *(30:4) Because God is infinite, certain things of his nature will always remain a mystery. These questions are similar to the questions God asked Job (Job, chapters 38-41) Some scholars believe that the Son referred to here is the Son of God, before the foundation of the earth, who participated in the creation.*

30:5-9 The believer replied: "Every word of God proves true; he protects everyone who runs to him for help. 6 Do not add to his

words, or he may reprimand you, and people will know you are a liar".
7 O God, I ask for two favors from you before I die. 8 First, keep me from telling lies and liars from my presence. Second, give me neither poverty nor riches. Give me only enough to live on. 9 For if I have too much, I might get independent and say, "God? Who needs him?" And if I'm too poor, I may steal and dishonor God's holy name.

> *(30:7-9) Either having too much or too little can be dangerous. Being poor can be a hazard to both spiritual and physical health. But, being rich is not the answer. Jesus pointed out that the rich will have trouble getting into heaven (Matthew 19:23-24). Our lives are more likely to be more effective if we have "neither poverty nor riches".*

30:10-17 Don't slander your fellow workers behind their backs; if you do the person will accuse you of being a backstabber and then you will be the guilty one. 11 Don't curse your father or fail to thank your mother. 12 Don't imagine yourself to be a pure one; you too, are not washed from your filthiness. 13 Don't be stuck up and think you are better than everyone else. 14 There is a generation that is greedy, merciless and cruel as wolves. They devour the poor with teeth as sharp as swords and shred the needy to pieces and discard them. 15 A leech has twin daughters named "Gimmie" and "Gimmie more." And there are three other things—no, four!—that are never satisfied:

> 16 the grave,
>   a womb incapable of producing offspring,
>   the thirsty dry land,
>   a blazing forest fire.

17 The eye that mocks his father or despises his mother will be plucked out by wild vultures and consumed by young eagles.

> *(30:13) This verse is referring to prideful and snobby people, who look down on others. Verses 11-14 contain descriptions of the arrogant.*

> *(30:15) "Three other things—no four", is a poetic way of saying the list is not complete. The writer is observing the world with delighted interest.*

30:18-33 There are three things that amaze me—no, four things I'll never understand:

> 19 how an eagle glides through the sky
> how a snake glides over a rock
> how a ship navigates the ocean
> and the way of a man with a young woman.

20 Equally amazing is how an adulterous woman can have sex with her client, shrug her shoulders, and then say, "Who's next?"

21 There are three things that are too much for even the earth to bear—no, four it cannot endure:

> 22 A slave who becomes a king,
> a fool who becomes rich.
> 23 A hateful woman who finally gets a husband,
> a girlfriend who replaces a faithful wife.

24 There are four things on earth that are small, but are exceedingly wise:
> 25 Ants—small and frail, but have plenty of food stored up for the winter.
> 26 Rock badgers are feeble; but they make their homes among the rocky cliffs.
> 27 Locusts—they have no king; yet they march like an army in ranks.
> 28 Lizards—easy enough to catch, but are found even in king's palaces.

> *Ants can teach us about preparation, **badgers** about wise building, **locusts** about cooperation and order, and **lizards** about fearlessness.*

29 There are three stately powers on earth—no, four:
> 30 the lion, king of the beasts, who doesn't turn away from anything.
> 31 a rooster, proud and strutting,
> a male goat,

a king whose troops are with him.

32 If you have been foolish enough to be prideful or to plot evil, don't brag about it. Instead, you should be covering your mouth with your hand in shame. 33 Churned milk turns into butter, a punch to the nose causes bleeding, and angry emotions turn into fights.

What lessons did you learn from this chapter?

_____

_____

_____

_____

_____

_____

_____

Chapter 31
SPEAK OUT FOR JUSTICE

The Words of King Lemuel's Mother

31:1-9 The words of King Lemuel, and the strong advice his mother gave him. 2 O my son, child whom I bore, the son I dedicated to God, 3 don't spend your strength on fortune-hunting women, on those who ruin kings. 4 It is not for kings, O Lemuel, to make a fool of themselves by gulping wine or for rulers to desire beer. 5 Otherwise, they may drink and forget their duties and unable to give justice to those who are afflicted. 6 Liquor is for those that are dying, and wine for those who are bitter of heart. 7 Let them drink to dull their pain, and for the terminally ill, for whom life is a living death. 8 Speak up for those who can't speak for themselves; for the rights of those who are down-and-out. 9 Speak out for justice! Stand up for the poor and helpless and make sure they get justice.

> *(31:4-7) Drunkenness is inexcusable for leaders of a nation, although it may be understandable among dying people in great pain. Alcohol impairs the mind and can lead to injustice and poor decision making. Those in leadership who ease their stress or pains with alcohol will eventually compromise their principals, which in turn, will affect their leadership abilities.*

A Wife of Noble Character

31:10-31 A woman of noble character is hard to find; and worth far more than diamonds. 11 Her husband can trust her without reserve; and he will not lack anything good. 12 She does him good and not evil, all the days of her life. 13 She shops around for the best yarns and cottons, and enjoys knitting and sewing. 14 She's like a merchant ship that sails to faraway places, and brings back exotic surprises. 15 She's up before dawn, prepares breakfast for her household and a portion for her maidservants. 16 She looks over a field and buys it; and with her earnings she plants a vineyard. 17 She is energetic and strong, and a hard worker. 18 She sees that her profits are good; and her lamp burns late into the night. 19 Her hands are skilled in spinning thread; her fingers twisting fiber. 20 She reaches out to help the poor; and she's quick to assist those in need. 21 She doesn't worry about her family in the winter, because their winter clothes are all mended and ready to wear. 22 She makes her own bed coverings; and dresses in colorful linens and silks. 23 Her husband is greatly respected, when he sits among the civic leaders of the land. 24 She makes linen garments and sells them; she delivers belts to the merchants. 25 Strength and dignity are her clothing; and she always faces tomorrow with a smile. 26 When she speaks, her words are wise; and when she gives instruction, she always speaks it kindly. 27 She carefully watches over her entire household, and is always busy and productive. 28 Her children respect and bless her. Her husband praises her: 29 "Many women have done wonderful things, but you have outclassed them all!" 30 Charm can be misleading, and beauty does not last; but a woman who fears the Lord is admired and praised. 31 Reward her for all she has done; adorn her life with praises!

(31:10-31) How fitting that the Book of Proverbs ends with the picture of a woman with strong character, great wisdom, many skills and compassion.
Some people have the mistaken idea that the ideal woman in the Bible is slavishly submissive and entirely domestic. This is not so! This woman is an excellent wife and mother. She's a manufacturer, manager, realtor, farmer, seamstress, upholsterer and merchant. Her strength and dignity are a result of her reverence for God. In today's society, physical appearance means so much, but notice, her appearance is never mentioned. Her attractiveness comes entirely from her character.
The woman described in this chapter has outstanding abilities and her family's social position is high. In fact, she may just be a composite portrait of ideal womanhood, and not one woman at all. Your days are not long enough to do everything she does, so don't see her as a model to imitate in every detail. Instead, see her as an inspiration to be all that you can be. We cannot be just like her, but we can learn from her integrity and resourcefulness.

What lessons did you learn from this chapter?

_____

_____

_____

_____

_____

_____

_____

REFERENCES:

Bible verses from the New Living Translation, New King James Version and the Message Bible, combined and reworded in a simple English format.

Explanations were written from research and interpretations from the author. Some explanation excerpts used in part from the New Living Translation (NLT)

Index By Word

"A"

ABOMINATION
6:16, 8:7, 11:1, 24:9, 28:9, 29:27

ACKNOWLEDGEMENT
3:6

ADULTERY
6:32

ADVISORS
11:14, 15:22

AFFLICTED
15:15

ANGER
15:1, 20:2, 22:24, 25:23, 29:22

ARROGANCE
8:13

"B"

BACKSLIDER
14:14

BETTER
15:16, 17:1, 19:1, 21:9, 21:19, 27:10

BITTERNESS
14:10

BORROWER
22:7

BROKEN
15:13, 17:22, 18:14

BROTHER
17:17, 18:19

"C"

CALAMITY
1:26, 6:15

CHARM
31:30

CHILDREN
20:7, 31:28

COMMIT
16:3

CONFESS
28:13

CONTEMPT
18:3

CORRECTION
3:11, 10:17, 12:1, 22:15, 23:13, 29:17

COUNSEL
1:25, 1:30, 11:14, 20:5, 20:18

COUNSELORS
11:14

CROOKED
2:15

CURSE
3:33, 26:2

<u>"D"</u>

DEATH
2:18, 8:36, 18:21

DECEIT
12:5, 12:20, 27:6

DECISION
16:33

DELIVER / DELIVERANCE
2:16, 21:31

DESIRES
19:22

DESPISES
11:12, 13:13, 14:21, 15:20

DESTRUCTION
10:29, 16:18, 18:12

DEVIOUS
2:15

DILIGENT
10:4, 12:24

DISCIPLINE
13:24, 15:10

<u>"E"</u>

ENEMY
25:21, 27:6

ENVY / ENVIOUS
14:30, 23:17, 24:1

EVIL
10:23, 12:21, 14:19, 15:3, 17:13, 31:12

EXTORTION
28:8

"F"

FAITHFUL
11:13, 20:6

FATHER
4:1

FAVOR
12:2, 19:12

FEAR
3:7, 29:25

FLATTERY
20:19, 26:28

FOLLY
15:21, 16:22

FOOL / FOOLS
1:7, 10:23, 11:29, 12:15, 13:16, 14:8, 14:9, 24:7

FOOLISH / FOOLISHNESS
9:6, 12:23, 14:1, 19:3, 21:20, 22:15, 24:9

FRIEND
14:20, 17:17, 18:24, 27:10

FURIOUS
22:24

"G"

GENEROUS
11:25, 22:9

GIFT / GIFTS
6:35, 18:16, 19:6, 21:14

GIVE
23:26, 28:27

GOOD
12:2, 12:25, 15:3, 17:22

GREEDY
1:19

"H"

HAPPY
3:13, 14:21, 16:20, 29:18

HATEFUL
30:23

HEART
15:13, 21:1, 23:7, 26:23, 27:19, 28:26

HELL
7:27, 23:14, 27:20

HOPE
23:18, 26:12

HUMILITY
22:4

"I"

IMPULSIVE
14:29

INSTRUCTION
1:7, 4:13, 8:33, 9:9, 12:1, 19:27, 23:12

"J"

JUSTICE
16:8, 28:5

"K"

KINDNESS
31:26

KNOWLEDGE
3:20, 8:10, 10:14, 14:6, 17:27, 19:2

"L"

LACK
28:27

LAZY
12:24, 12:27, 13:4, 19:24, 24:30, 26:16

LEARN / LEARNING
1:5, 22:25

LIFE
2:19, 3:18, 3:22, 8:35, 15:24, 29:24

LOVE
7:18, 10:12, 17:17

LUST
6:25, 11:6

LYING
13:5

"M"

MERCY
3:3, 14:31

MOCK / MOCKER
1:26, 14:9, 17:5, 20:1

MOUTH
10:14, 13:3, 22:14, 26:28

"N"

NATION
14:34

NEGLECT
1:8, 6:20

"O"

OBEDIENCE
6:20

OFFENSE
10:12

"P"

PERISH
14:11, 31:8

PERVERSE
4:24, 6:14

PLEASANT
2:10, 3:17, 16:24

PLEASURE
21:17

POOR
10:4, 14 :20, 14:21, 14:31, 17 :5, 19:22, 22:2, 22:22, 28:3, 28:6

POVERTY
20:13, 21:5

PRAISE
27:2, 31:28

PRIDE
8:13, 13:10, 16:18, 29:23

PROUD
15:25, 16:5, 28:25

PURE
15:26, 16:2, 20:9, 21:8, 30:12

"Q"

QUARREL
17:19, 20:3

QUICK-TEMPERED
14:17

"R"

REBELLION
17:11

REBUKE
1:23, 9:8, 15:31, 17:10, 28:23

REWARD
11:18, 25:22

RICH / RICHES
3:16, 8:18, 11:25, 11:28, 13:7, 14:20, 14:24, 19:14, 22:2, 22:4, 22:7, 27:24, 28:11

RIGHTEOUS
10:3, 10:11, 10:16, 10:28, 11:8, 11:21, 11:28, 11:31, 12:10, 12:26, 15:6, 15:29, 18:10, 28:1, 29:2, 29:7

RIGHTEOUSNESS
10:2, 11:5, 11:6, 11:19, 12:28, 13:6, 14:34, 16:31, 21:21

"S"

SATISFIED
12:11, 14:14, 27:7, 30:15

SERVANT
11:29, 17:2, 29:19

SHAME
10:5

SIN
1:10, 8:36, 14:34

SLEEP
3:24, 4:16, 6:10, 10:5, 20:13

SORROW
10:22, 14:13

SOUL
6:32, 8:36, 19:2, 27:7

STRENGTH
10:29, 24:5, 31:25

STRIFE
10:12, 13:10, 15:18, 17:19

<u>**"T"**</u>

THIEF
6:30, 29:24

TONGUE
10:31, 12:19, 15:4, 21:23, 25:15

TROUBLE
11:8, 15:6

TRUST
3:5

<u>**"U"**</u>

UNDERSTAND (*ING*)
2:2, 3:5, 3:19, 9:6, 9:10, 10:23, 14:8, 16:22, 19:8, 23:23, 28:5, 28:11

UNFAITHFUL
2:22, 13:15

UNPUNISHED
11:21, 28:20

<u>**"W"**</u>

WEALTH
10:15, 13:11, 19:4

WICKED
2:22, 11:5, 15:29

WINE
20:1, 23:31

WISDOM
3:13, 4:5, 4:7, 9:10, 16:16, 19:8, 24:7

WISE
3:7, 11:30, 16:21, 26:5, 30:24